# By A

# © Copyright 2015

# Disclaimer

The information provided in this book is designed to provide helpful information on the subjects discussed. The author's books are only meant to provide the reader with the basics knowledge of a certain topic, without any warranties regarding whether the student will, or will not, be able to incorporate and apply all the information provided. Although the writer will make his best effort share his insights, learning is a difficult task and each person needs a different timeframe to fully incorporate a new topic. This book, nor any of the author's books constitute a promise that the reader will learn a certain topic within a certain timeframe.

# LEARN SQL IN A DAY

## The Ultimate Crash Course to Learning the Basics of SQL in No Time

# Table of Contents

# Chapter 1 – Introduction to SQL

**Chapter Objective:** Understand why SQL is important, why you need to know it, and what it's used for. This chapter is mainly an introduction to SQL and its purpose in web programming and design.

Whether you want to just own a website or get into the nitty gritty of web design and programming, you will undoubtedly need to know SQL. Structured Query Language (SQL) is the language of databases. There are different flavors of the language depending on the platform that you use. This eBook will focus on the MySQL platform, but there are slight differences between T-SQL (Microsoft) and PL-SQL (Oracle). As long as you learn one platform, you can intelligently write SQL code for other platforms.

**Why You Need to Use SQL?**

In the 1990s, webmasters could use just static HTML page. A static HTML page displays information to the viewer without changing content. If you had a list of products to display, you had to code HTML for each of these products on the page. If you added a new product, you had to recode the page to add your new product. This could get tedious if you have thousands of products.

SQL lets you dynamically create web pages. You can have 1000 products in your database, and SQL allows you to use a few lines of code to display it on the page. You must you a dynamic language on your server, but this eBook focuses on the backend database SQL language.

Currently, most dynamic web pages use some form of SQL. No other solution offers the security, performance, and resilience of a SQL platform. You could use a list of products in a file and upload it to your server, but this method does not have the security and performance of a SQL database.

For this reason, you need SQL if you want to manage or create web pages. Understanding web programming and SQL go hand-in-hand. You can't code a dynamic web page without running across some form of SQL. For programmers, understanding SQL is a must-have in an arsenal of coding languages. For webmasters, understanding SQL greatly improves their understanding of the way their website is managed. Knowing SQL will even help average webmasters who know a little bit about code to fix their own problems instead of relying on a third-party.

Another reason to know SQL is troubleshooting issues. For instance, your web page only displays 100 products out of 1000 you've stored in a database. To troubleshoot this issue, you first look at your database SQL coding to understand if the root cause is indeed caused by the database programming.

You might want a quick report on the performance of your sales funnel. You might want to see a list of customers and their associated orders. You would do this using the SQL language directly in your database. SQL has several uses, and webmasters should understand its use when they need to manage a customized website.

**What is SQL Used For?**

SQL is used to make your website dynamic.

We briefly mentioned in the previous section why you would use SQL. SQL is the standard for dynamic websites, but what exactly does that mean?

There are four main functions of the SQL language: Read, Write, Update, and Delete. It seems simple, but these statements can get advanced as your website and database grow. Let's take a look at these four functions and see what they are used for.

## Read

You can't do much with a database if you can't read the data. The SELECT statement is the SQL language's "read" statement. It lets you retrieve records and review them. Your website code retrieves records to display them to the end user (your customers). Any report uses a SELECT statement to read and calculate your data.

## Write

At some point, you need to write data to your database. When a customer signs up with a new account, you write the customer's information to the database and store it in your tables. The write command is the INSERT statement in SQL. The INSERT command stores data in your tables, so you can read it later.

## Update

What happens when your customer accidentally misspells his name? You need to allow that customer to change the information stored in the database. You do this using the UPDATE statement. This statement allows you and your website users to change the stored information in database tables.

## Delete

The final statement in the SQL language is the DELETE statement. This statement removes a record from the database. You must consider constraints, which we will explain in future chapters, or you risk creating orphaned records. Some database administrators reject the idea of ever deleting records in your database. For auditing and security reasons, it's generally frowned on to delete records, but there are times when you need to use the DELETE statement for managing your records and information.

Put these four statements together, and you have everything you need to work with your data. It might seem simple for such a huge, complex platform, but these four functions are all you need to work with a SQL platform. Before you learn the language or build your site, you first need to understand which platform is right for you.

## Choosing a SQL Platform

Several database systems use the SQL language. A SQL database is the foundation and work horse for your site. Once you ingrain a platform into your website, you are stuck with this platform. It's very costly and time-consuming to change your database platform, so you should choose the system that works best for you. The backend language you use has a lot to do with your choices, but most mainstream languages work with any SQL platform. We'll cover the three main database platforms, but you have several others to choose from on the market. If you're a new business, you should probably stick to a tried and true platform. Well-known platforms usually have better support from communities and vendors.

## MySQL

MySQL is the platform we'll focus on as we discuss the SQL language. MySQL is an open-source database that powers several big companies. It's also the main database platform that works with common pre-packaged solutions such as WordPress. MySQL has a majority of the database market, because it's free for developers and website owners, and it has a great support community where anyone can ask questions and get help. Corporations that need a higher level of support pay for a subscription. This is how open-source platforms such as MySQL make their revenue.

SQL Server

Microsoft SQL Server is a main database platform for Windows environments. If you choose to write a website based in a Microsoft language such as C# or VB.NET, you would probably work with SQL Server. SQL Server integrates with Windows and Microsoft technology very well, and its T-SQL language is what powers your database queries. Microsoft is not open-source, and this platform can be more expensive for a startup. MySQL and SQL Server programmers are able to configure and work with each database since many of the commands are similar.

Oracle

The Oracle database platform has been around for decades. It's usually a high-end, high-traffic work horse for bigger companies. Oracle uses the PL-SQL language, which is much more different than other languages. If you work with Java or large business environments, you will probably run into an Oracle database. Oracle has the smallest market share for general purpose websites because of its price.

There are several other platforms on the market including PostgreSQL, MongoDB, and even small personal systems such as Access. You might need some consulting if you are building a new website, but most developers work with either MySQL or SQL Server.

## How is SQL Used in Business?

SQL is used in several industries. It's also used with internal systems. If you own a business or work with any type of website, you'll probably need to know SQL. You already know that SQL is used to create dynamic websites, but it's used in several other business applications.

First, if you need to build an internal customer relationship management system (CRM), you need to work with SQL. SQL manages each customer transaction, customer service tickets, and order and shipping management. Data is stored in tables, which we will cover in chapter 2. The data is manipulated and retrieved using SQL.

You also need SQL for reporting. A SQL database usually runs on a very powerful computer, so reports should be fast. For bigger companies, a separate SQL database is used specifically for reporting, so large reports don't slow down the main production database.

In this eBook, we will cover all aspects of SQL that you need to know to begin developing websites, reports, or to simply query your database for data. We show you the importance of tables and storing your data. We cover the four main functions we described in the previous sections. You will learn how to read, write, edit and delete your data.

One final note about SQL and MySQL: MySQL is a relational database. This means that each table has related data to other tables. We get into tables and relationships in the next chapter, but it's important to note that MySQL does not just store data in an unorganized fashion. You must create tables that organize data in a way that allows the database to build relationships between these tables.

SQL is mostly queries, so we show you how to write more advanced queries by joining your tables, aggregating data, using cursors to loop through data, and security your applications. Our final chapters give you a small introduction to coding PHP with a MySQL database backend. You'll get to see SQL at work and work with real-life solutions.

## Lab Questions

1. When you want to read data from the database, what command do you use?
    a. SELECT
    b. UPDATE
    c. DELETE
    d. INSERT
Explanation: the SELECT statement is the read statement for SQL in any database engine.

2. What open-source database platform is preferred for its low cost and free availability for webmasters?
    a. Oracle
    b. SQL Server
    c. MySQL
    d. IIS
Explanation: MySQL is affordable and works with most application languages.

3. When you want to add a record to the database tables, what SQL command do you use?

     a. SELECT
     b. UPDATE
     c. DELETE
     d. INSERT

Explanation: the INSERT statement adds a record to a table. It's a write command when you set up SQL permissions.

4. When you want to delete a record from a database, what SQL command do you use?

     a. SELECT
     b. UPDATE
     c. DELETE
     d. INSERT

Explanation: the DELETE statement removes a record from a table.

5. When you want to edit the data in a table, what SQL command do you use?

     a. SELECT
     b. UPDATE
     c. DELETE
     d. INSERT

Explanation: the UPDATE statement is used to edit and change data in your table records.

# Chapter 2 – Tables

**Chapter Objective:** This chapter explains the relationship between data and tables. Tables are storage holders for your data. We explain tables and explain how to conceptualize how they store data.

Tables are database objects that store your data. You design the tables, so the quality of your database design depends on your ability to understand tables, relationships, and data integrity. Poorly designed tables can greatly reduce performance on your database, so it's important to understand the way tables work and how you should create them.

**Understanding a Database Table Structure**

The best way to understand and learn a table design is to think of a table as a large spreadsheet. Most people have experience with spreadsheet software such as Excel, and knowing this software will help you as you learn table structure.

Think of how a spreadsheet is laid out. You have columns and rows, and where these two items intercept is called a field. A table is laid out with the same type of structure. You create column names when you create your tables. For instance, if you need to store a list of customers, you would create a "first_name" and "last_name" column. Notice that we used underscores instead of spaces in the table name. This is standard for naming procedures.

Each record you insert creates a new row. Think of the customer table example again. You insert a new customer named "James Smith." "James" inserts into the first_name column, and "Smith" inserts into the last_name column. Combined these two fields make one record or one row.

**Understanding Primary and Foreign Keys**

As you understand tables and relationships better, you'll get to read table data more efficiently. Just think of each table as a separate spreadsheet. The main difference is that each table has a relationship with each other. We mentioned relational data in the previous chapter, and we'll help you understand its structure in this chapter.

Let's go back to the customer example. You have a table with a list of customers. You can't put all data into one table. You need to create tables that match the different components of your application. Let's say you need to store a list of orders. You can't store orders as one record with your customer, because multiple orders could be linked to one customer. When you can have multiple records for one matching record, you break out your table to a second table. In this example, we want to make an Order table.

However, we need to ensure that each Order table record can be linked with a customer record. We place a foreign key in the Order table to link a customer with an order. Here is a better representation of the Order and Customer tables.

Customer
----------------------------
customer_id, first_name, last_name


Order

----------------------------
order_id, customer_id, product_name

Notice that each table has an id column. This column is an autoincrementing number that creates a unique part of the record. MySQL will keep track of autoincrementing numbers, so you don't need to. The database takes the last record and increments it by 1. The result is that you have a unique field for each record, which is what you need to identify a customer or an order.

Notice that the Order table has the customer_id field. This is the link we spoke about earlier. This links the customer with the order. Your entire table structure and layout will use these links to join relationships between tables.

The id fields are the primary keys for the table. A primary key must be a unique field in the table. We used an autoincrementing numeric field, so the value is always unique since MySQL automatically increments the number. When you learn to query this data, you'll learn that this field will let you uniquely identify the record as you update, retrieve or delete it.

The customer_id field in the Order table is considered the foreign key. The primary-foreign key relationship is what makes a relational database. It's what links your tables to the primary table. The foreign key usually has the same name as the field in the primary table, but a database isn't always built that way. The naming scheme usually depends on the database designer unless certain standards are given to the developer.

# Creating Tables

Now that you have an understanding of tables, layout and relationships, you need to know how to create those tables. The SQL language has a specific statement for creating tables. The statement can get complex, but we just need to create a new customer table. We're going to create a table to store our customers. We know that we need a customer first and last name and an id to store the unique, autoincrementing numeric primary key.

Take a look at the following SQL statement:

```
CREATE TABLE Customer (
customer_id INT(6) AUTO_INCREMENT PRIMARY KEY,
first_name VARCHAR(30),
last_name VARCHAR(30)
);
```

The CREATE TABLE statement defines the columns for your table. The first column is an integer, and as you can see from the statement, it's autoincrementing and set as the primary key. The next two statements are the first and last name columns. The SQL language uses the VARCHAR statement to indicate that the column should hold a variable string. The first name could be 5 characters or it could be 30. The "30" statement tells the database that the maximum number of characters that the column can hold is 30 characters. Make sure you allow the column to have plenty of characters to support your application. If you enter a first name that's 40 characters, the database truncates the value and gives your application a warning.

You'll notice in all of our example SQL statements that a semicolon is used at the end of the statement.

You need this character to indicate to MySQL that the end of a statement is reached. With SQL Server T-SQL, you do not need to include the semicolon. This is one minor difference between SQL platforms.

Let's create an Order table to keep track of customer orders. The following statement creates an Order table for your table design.

```
CREATE TABLE Order (
order_id INT(6) AUTO_INCREMENT PRIMARY KEY,
customer_id INT(6),
product_name VARCHAR(30),
FOREIGN KEY (customer_id) REFERENCES
Customer(customer_id)
);
```

Notice that we again create a primary key for the order_id column, and then we have the customer_id column set as a foreign key. To create a constraint between the primary and foreign keys, you must specify which column is the foreign key and what it references.

You might wonder why you would create a constraint at all. A constraint links tables, but it also stops you from creating orphaned records. For instance, suppose you have 2 orders linked to 1 customer. You decide to delete the customer record. The Order table no longer has a customer reference. The result is that your orders are referenced. For applications, this results in data integrity issues and usually errors in your application. With a primary-foreign constraint set up, you are not able to delete the customer without first deleting the order records. The result is better data integrity for your database.

## Altering Table Structure

You can't expect to build a table perfectly during your first round of design. Even if you do, future enhancements to your application will require you to add columns to the table. Whatever changes you decide to make to your table, you'll need to use the ALTER TABLE statement.  This statement lets you make changes to the database structure whether it's a change to primary or foreign keys, changes in data type for a column or adding a new column – you'll need to know the ALTER TABLE statement.

For instance, let's say you want to add an order_total column to the Order table. You forgot to include this column in the original CREATE TABLE statement, so you need to add a new column. The following SQL statement adds your new column.

ALTER TABLE Order ADD order_total decimal(4,2);

Notice that we didn't need to redefine the columns we already created in the CREATE TABLE statement. We just need to use the ALTER TABLE statement with the ADD statement to add a new column. Since order totals usually need decimal values, we set the value to decimal to include precision in our table design. The "4" value tells MySQL that the value can be up to four digits, and the "2" indicates that MySQL should keep a precision up to two decimals.

## Deleting Tables

While it's not advisable, you sometimes need to delete tables. In typical environments, you would not delete a table unless you knew beyond a shadow of a doubt that you do not reference the table anywhere in your application or database commands.

As your database grows, you can't guarantee that there is no reference at all to a table, so most database administrators leave tables active instead of deleting them. When you delete a table, you also delete the data, so you can understand why this might be a problem.

Nonetheless, you should still understand how to delete a table in case you need to rid the system of the object.

When you need to delete a table, you use the DROP TABLE statement. For instance, suppose you decide to delete your Order table, the following command applies.

DROP TABLE Order;

That's it – your table is gone along with any of its data. If you change your mind, you need to restore the data and the table structure from your database backup. This can be time consuming, and a table deleted by mistake can cripple your application. Some database administrators test the need for the table by renaming it. If something goes wrong when the table is renamed, then you rename the table back to its original name. In both ways, it can be a critical error on the database administrator's part, so always delete tables with care.

**Chapter Summary**

Tables are the main storage components for your database. Most people must sit down and map out tables and database design. This will save you time when you need several tables and aren't sure how to design them. Draw your design on a whiteboard or on paper, and then use the CREATE TABLE and ALTER TABLE statements to create your tables. This chapter covered the basics, but it can take weeks to design a large repository of tables.

## Lab Questions

1. You decide you want to add a column to an existing table named Order. You want to add a new column named order_estimate. What is the correct statement?
A. ALTER TABLE Order ADD order_estimate decimal(4,2);
B. ALTER TABLE Order INSERT order_total decimal(4,2);
C. CREATE TABLE Order ADD order_estimate decimal(4,2);
D. CREATE TABLE INSERT order_estimate decimal(4,2);
Explanation: You use the ALTER TABLE with the ADD statement to add a new column to the table.

2. You decide to create a new Product table. You want to create the table with two columns named product_id and product_name. Write the correct statement to create the table.
Answer:
CREATE TABLE Product (
product_id INT(6) AUTO_INCREMENT PRIMARY KEY,
product_name VARCHAR(30)
);
Explanation: The CREATE TABLE statement creates a new table object. You must define your columns and the column data types to properly set up the statement.

3. You decide you want to delete the Product table you just created. You know that nothing refers to the Product table, so you confirm that you can delete the table. Write the proper delete statement for a table.
Answer:
DROP TABLE Product;
Explanation: the DROP TABLE statement completely deletes both the table structure and the table data.

# Chapter 3 – User Variables

**Chapter Objective:** This chapter helps you understand the concepts of user defined variables, which are variables you use in stored procedures and customized SQL scripts. After reading this chapter, readers should understand how to create variables and assign values for SQL scripts.

Just like any other programming language, SQL gives you the ability to create your own variables. These variables contain values that you assign to them. Values can be from a table, statically defined, or input from an external application. They are named "variables," because they can contain any number of values. What a variable contains is completely up to the programmer. The only restriction you have is the data type used when you define the user variable, which we will also discuss in this chapter.

**User Defined Variable Basics**

When you define a user variable, it's only good for a specific session. If you're familiar with programming concepts, a computer assigns a user defined variable a chunk of memory space when the program runs. When the program finishes, the memory is released. The same is true for user variables in SQL. When your stored procedure or SQL statement runs, the user variable is given memory space, and when the statements are finished, the memory is released.

This is an important factor, because you won't be able to retrieve your user variable values after the SQL statement runs.

Another important basic factor is how variables are constructed. Every programming language has its own standards and restrictions when naming variables, and SQL is no different.

First, your user defined variables must start with the @ symbol. This tells the SQL language that you're creating a variable. System variables also start with the @ symbol, but a good user interface and programming environment color codes these variables, so you can quickly see the difference.

Second, a user variable cannot contain all special characters. The only special characters you can use are the dollar sign, underscores and a period. For the most part, database administrators stick to alphanumeric user defined variable names with underscores to separate words. In rare cases you might see a dollar sign or a period, but most variables are alphanumeric. You can use any letter of the alphabet and any number in your variable names.

There is one exception to this rule. If you use quotes around your variable names, you can use special characters. This is not common practice, though, since it adds to programming complexity and means any time the variable is used, you must ensure that it uses quotes.

**Defining User Variables**

With naming conventions in mind, you can now practice creating user defined variables.

Let's take a look at an example. Let's define a variable for our customer's first name.

```
SET @first_name = 'john';
SELECT @first_name;
```

The SET statement is used to create a user defined variable and assign it a value. In this example, a @first_name variable is created and assigned the value 'john'. Notice the semicolon at the end of the SET statement. The semicolon is required to terminate your statements. You can have very long SQL statements that need more than one line on your screen to complete. In this case, the SQL compiler would know when the multi-line statement is finished – the semicolon. If you excluded the semicolon, the SQL database engine will give you an error. In other words, always remember to include the semicolon at the end of your SQL statements.

With the SELECT statement, you see the following output.

@first_name
--------------------------------
john

You might ask yourself why we included the SELECT statement with our example. You can define a user variable and assign it a variable, but SQL doesn't automatically display the value back to you. To test your new variable, you need to use the SELECT statement. We'll get more detailed with SELECT statements in future chapters. For this chapter, suffice to say that the SELECT statement retrieves values and displays them to you.

You don't need to define a variable one-by-one. You can also choose to define several variables at once. Take a look at the following user variable definition.

SET @first_name = 'john', @last_name = 'smith';
SELECT @first_name, @last_name;

Just like the first statement, we define a first name variable for our customer. In this statement, however, we add a variable for the customer's last name. You can define multiple user variables in one statement by just separating each variable using a comma.

The above statements produce the following output.

@first_name, @last_name
------------------------------------------------
john   smith

In some instances, you need to combine multiple user variables into one. When you do this, you need to use the := assignment variable. If you attempt to use the equal character like we used in previous examples, the SQL engine sees this as a comparison operator rather than an assignment operator.

Let's look at a sample.

SET @first_name = 'john', @last_name = 'smith', @full_name := @first_name + ' ' + @last_name;
SELECT @first_name, @last_name, @full_name;

You see the following output.

@first_name, @last_name, @full_name
-----------------------------------------------------------
john   smith john smith

In the above example, we still have the first and last name variables. We've added one more named @full_name. This variable contains the concatenation of the first and last name with a space in between.

Notice that we used the := assignment operator. You need this operator when you're using multiple values to assign values to one variable when you defined your variables.
Incidentally, you can use the := assignment operator with other assignments. The following SQL statements are also valid.

```
SET @first_name := 'john', @last_name := 'smith', @full_name
:= @first_name + ' ' + @last_name;
SELECT @first_name, @last_name, @full_name;
```

The above statements produce the same output as before.

```
@first_name, @last_name, @full_name
----------------------------------------------------------
john    smith  john smith
```

When you use the := assignment operator, you ensure that SQL is always assigning values to variables instead of using a comparison operator.

We've used string values up until this point, so let's take a look at some numerical values. You can assign numerical values to your user defined variables too. Let's take a look at an example.

```
SET @order_price = 35.00;
SELECT @order_price;
```

The output is what you would expect. The following output is displayed.

```
@order_price
--------------------------------
35.00
```

You can also add values and display them for your application or on your screen. The following is another example.

```
SET @order_price = 35, @order_total := @order_price + 10.00;
SELECT @order_price, @order_total;
```

Notice again at the assignment operators. If we used the equal sign to add up our order total, the SQL engine would give us an error. The following output is shown to the user.

```
@order_price, @order_total
---------------------------------
35.00          45.00
```

The SQL engine knows to add values and provide 45.00 as the output instead of concatenating strings like the previous string values. This is because we first gave our user variables string values, and then we gave them decimal values. It's important to keep your data types defined to avoid any errors or bugs in your application. If you attempt to add incompatible values together such as a decimal and an integer, you run the risk of introducing bugs to your system.

You can also use variables to assign values from tables. If you recall from the previous chapter, we discussed table structure. Let's assume we have a customer table with a first and last name column. We want to extract the first name of one of our customers in this table. Again, we'll discuss the SELECT statement soon, but let's take a look at how we extract the column information using a user defined variable.

```
SELECT @first_name := first_name FROM Customer WHERE
customer_id = 1;
SELECT @first_name;
```

In this example, the first name for customer with an ID of 1 is stored in the @first_name variable. The result is the following data set.

```
@first_name,
----------------------------------------------------------
john
```

The output, as you can see, is just the same as if you had statically assigned the variable value.

What if you don't know what to assign to a variable? The SQL language uses a value called NULL. The NULL value can be stored in tables and variables. If you attempt to retrieve data from a table and the value doesn't exist, the SQL engine automatically assigns the value of NULL. You shouldn't consider a NULL value as "nothing." The NULL value is indeed a value, but it's a container that tells your applications that there is no value available.

Database administrators use NULL values to assign variables an initial value when they don't know what to assign initially. Let's take a look at an example.

```
SET @first_name = NULL;
SELECT @first_name;
SELECT @first_name := first_name FROM Customer WHERE customer_id = 1;
```

The output is the following.

```
@first_name
-----------------------------
NULL
```

```
@first_name
```

--------------------------------

John

Notice that there are two output blocks. That's because we have two SELECT statements. The first variable assignment is set to NULL because we don't know what to use as a value. The next statement pulls the variable value from a table named Customer. The value assigned is the first name of a customer with the ID of 1. In our example, the first name is John, so it's printed to the output screen.

These highlights are the basics of user variables. When you work with applications and reports, you will run into several user variables. You will need to create user variables in any application, because you can't use static variables throughout any dynamic interface. These user variables are typically used when you take input from a user, but they are also useful when you need to extract information from tables and return them to an application or report.

In this chapter, we gave you the overview and a basic understanding of user variables. They are one of the easier concepts to understand, but they are important factors when working with SQL programming. Remember that these variables are only available in one session. If you assign a variable value in a SQL statement and later come back for that variable value, the SQL engine returns NULL. In other words, you can't run one of these SQL statements in one stored procedure and then retrieve the same value in a second stored procedure. This concept can be difficult for new developers to understand, but you start to understand once you get more practice.

Let's practice some of what we just learned in a lab.

## Lab Questions

1. When you assign values to a user variable, what operator should you use to avoid confusion and errors with the comparison operator?

A. =

B. ==

C. :=

D. !=

Explanation: this assignment operator leaves no errors when you create multiple user variables and their values.

2. You decide to create a user variable for a product name to later insert that product name into a table. Write the statement that would create a variable named @product_table and assign it the value of NULL.

SET @product_name = NULL;

3. You want to read a value you just assigned to a variable named @product_name. Write your SELECT statement to retrieve the value of a variable and display it on your screen.

SELECT @product_name;

4. What character is used to terminate all SQL statements?

A. :

B. ;

C. ::

D. @

Explanation: use the exclamation mark to terminate your SQL statements. You can use multiple lines in your code, and SQL understands that the semicolon is the end of the statement.

# Chapter 4 – Reading Data

**Chapter Objective:** Storing data in your tables is the first step when working with databases, but you must be able to retrieve and read the data. This chapter shows you how to read the data you've stored in your SQL tables.

With an understanding of tables covered in chapter 2, it's time to understand how to retrieve that data from your tables. The SQL language uses the SELECT statement to retrieve data. You saw this statement in the previous chapter to display a user defined variable value. You use the same statement to retrieve and review table data.

If you recall, a table is made up of columns and rows. The columns are the field names for your data such as first or last name. The rows are your records. If you have 10 customers in a customer table that lists a first and last name, you have 10 records and 2 columns. Remember to view your tables like you view a spreadsheet.

## The Basic SELECT Syntax

You were introduced last chapter to the SELECT statement. Let's take a look at the general syntax.

SELECT item;

That's the only requirement for a SELECT statement. In this instance, you need to define "item." In the previous chapter, this item was a user variable. In this chapter, we'll focus on retrieving data from tables, so you need more in your SELECT statement.

The following syntax is the template for querying tables.

SELECT column_name FROM table;

In this statement, we identify a column in the table named table. Just like user variables, you can use one or several columns when you retrieve your data. Let's take the template and use it for querying our customer table.

The following statement gets the first name of all customers in the Customer table.

SELECT first_name FROM Customer;

Notice that first_name does not have the @ symbol prefixed. This is because the table column is not a user variable, and only user variables require the @ symbol. In this example, we retrieve all first name values from the Customer table. Let's assume you have two customers in the table. Take a look at the output.

```
first_name
-------------------------------
John
Jane
```

You have two records and returned one column for each record.

SQL gives you the option to return all columns for a specific table. The asterisk character can be used to retrieve all columns without explicitly telling the SQL engine what columns to return. It's not recommended for performance reasons, but you should know how to perform the query and how to identify it if you ever review someone else's SQL statements.

Take a look at the following query.

SELECT * FROM Customer;

In the above statement, we tell the SQL engine to return all columns. Again, it's not recommended by useful if you want to do a quick check on your data. The above query returns the following output.

customer_id, first_name, last_name
-------------------------------
1       John   Smith
2       Jane   Johnson

With the asterisk character, we now know that the Customer table contains three columns. The first column is the ID, and the second and third columns are the customer first and last name. If you add another column to a table, the new column with display in the results without you knowing the column name.

We will avoid using the asterisk symbol to display all columns in a query result set since it's not recommended.

**Filtering Data**

The above examples showed you how to retrieve records, but the results showed all records.

What happens when your table grows to thousands of customers? You need a way to filter only customers that you want to see. You do this using the WHERE clause. The WHERE clause is SQL's filter.

Let's start with a simple statement. Let's get all customers that have a first name of 'John' using the WHERE clause. The following is the example SQL that retrieves results.

SELECT first_name, last_name FROM Customer WHERE first_name = 'john';

You'll notice the SELECT statement syntax template we mentioned earlier. The customer's first and last name columns are returned. The difference in the above statement is that only a subset of records in the Customer table is returned. We only have one record with the first name of John. The following result set is displayed.

first_name, last_name
---------------------------------------------
John    Smith

Notice instead of showing one record, SQL only returns one. That's the magic of the WHERE clause filter. You're not only limited to just one filter either. You're able to use several statements in your SELECT query to filter on multiple fields. If no records match, the SQL engine returns no records.

Let's take a look at what happens if you query on two fields and no records are returned.

SELECT first_name, last_name FROM Customer WHERE first_name = 'john' and customer_id = 2;

The "and" keyword separates your WHERE clause filters. You can have one or several and statements for your WHERE clause. As long as you continue to use the and clause, the SQL engine continues to add more filters to the result set. In the above statement, the SQL statement is looking for customers with an id of 2 and a first name of John. If you recall from previous SELECT statements, the customer with the first name of John has an ID of 1. That means nothing matches once you combine both WHERE clause filters.

The following is your result set displayed.

first_name, last_name
------------------------------------------

Notice that no records were returned. This is distinct from a record set that returns NULL values. Remember, NULL is a value, so any fields that contain a NULL value are returned.

You can also query based on the NULL value. Let's assume that our John customer didn't input his last name when he signed up to our website. You allow NULL values to store in your table, so the last name is filled with the NULL value in your database table. You want to find out how many of your customers chose not to input a last name. You want to query the last name for any NULL values.

The following SQL statement shows you how to filter on NULL values.

SELECT first_name, last_name FROM Customer WHERE last_name IS NULL;

Notice that we used the keywords IS NULL in the statement instead of the equal sign. This is an important piece of information when working with database table information. Note that NULL never equates or compares to any other value. Using the equal sign in this instance would return no records even if you indeed had records with a last name of NULL. The SQL language uses "IS NULL" or "IS NOT NULL" when comparing NUL values. The first phrase returns any records that contain NULL values, and the second phrase returns any records the do not have a NULL value. This type of query is often used by database administrators to identify any missing data, especially if it's critical for an application.

You can use other comparison operators to search a SQL database. Let's say you want to query your Order table for all orders that are greater than $10. The dollar sign isn't stored in the database, but the database stores a decimal value of 10.00. You can identify which orders are greater than 10 using the greater than operator or >.

The following SQL statement searches for orders with a total amount greater than 10.

SELECT order_id, product_name FROM Order WHERE total > 10;

The result could look like the following if the result returns records.

order_id, product_name
-----------------------------------------
33      My Service

In this example, you have an order with the ID of 33 in the database. Although we don't print out the total order amount, we can assume that the order total amount is greater than 10.

In the above statement, it's important to note that the query only returns values that are more than 10. If you have an order that is 10.00, it does not return the record. If you want to return all records that are more than 10 and records that are equal to 10, you want to use the greater than or equal to operation or >=.

Let's change the operator in our order query.

SELECT order_id, product_name FROM Order WHERE total >= 10;

Let's assume we have a record that includes a 10 order total. You would see the following output.

order_id, product_name
----------------------------------------
33      My Service
10      My Other Service

You also have other operators you can choose from. You can use less than < or less than and equal to. <=. These two operators would have the effect that you would imagine – all records that are less than or less than and equal to be returned.

What if you only want to see records that don't equal a specific value? For instance, you want all records that don't have an order total of 10. You just want to include all but one value in your record set. You can use the "not equal to" or != operator.

Let's take a look at a sample.

SELECT order_id, product_name FROM Order WHERE total != 10;

Instead of including all records that have an order total of 10, you now exclude all of these records. The following output uses are data from previous query results.

order_id, product_name

----------------------------------------

33      My Service
10      My Discount Offer

We still get the order that has a total over 10, but now we see another record. We can assume from the previous logic that order ID 10 has a total value less than 10 since it did not show up in our first record set.

As you work with SQL and any database engine, you'll see the SELECT statement several times in your code. You'll need to know how to use the SELECT statement any time you want to review records, and applications such as PHP use the SELECT statement frequently to retrieve data to display to your users.

Practice with the SELECT statement on your database to get some practice. The SELECT statement is relatively harmless since you do not edit any data when you run the query. For this reason, it's the best SQL statement to use for beginners just getting started with the language.

Let's take a look at some lab questions to help you practice with SELECT statements.

## Lab Questions

1. You want to find customers who didn't enter a last name. Write the SQL statement that would find all customers with a last name of NULL.
SELECT customer_id FROM Customers WHERE last_name IS NULL;

Explanation: the above statement returns a list of customers where the last name is set as NULL. Notice the IS NULL syntax and not the equal operator used for NULL values.

2. You want to find all orders where the total is greater than $50. You don't want to include $50 orders. You only want orders that are greater than $50. Write the SQL statement that would display correct results.

SELECT order_id FROM Order WHERE order_total > 50;

Explanation: the greater than sign is used to find all orders greater than 50. If you wanted to get orders that include 50 totals, you would use the >= operator.

3. What character lets you return all columns in a table without specifying columns to return in a SELECT statement?

A. *
B. @
C. #
D. %

Explanation: the asterisk symbol lets you return all columns, but it's not recommended for performance reasons.

4. You want to review all orders that don't have a 0 total value. Write the query that would return all records that don't have a 0 value.

SELECT order_id, product_name FROM Order WHERE total != 0;

The above query gets all orders that don't have a total of 0. The != operator means "does not equal."

# Chapter 5 – Deleting Data

**Chapter Objective:** This chapter covers the basics of removing records from your database tables. It's not recommended, but you should still know how to delete data. This chapter covers the SQL DELETE statement.

While you want to avoid deleting data in your database, there are times you need to remove records. For instance, suppose you accidentally import duplicate records and have no way to deactivate them unless you delete them. You could use the SQL DELETE statement to remove records from your tables. You'll also need to edit stored procedures with the DELETE statement, so it's an important part of SQL that you should know.

**DELETE Statement Basics**

Just like the SELECT statement in the previous statement, the DELETE statement also has a basic template. While reading data from your tables is relatively harmless, you can cause serious data integrity issues when you accidentally delete records. For this reason, you only want to run DELETE statements on test data until you are confident it can be moved into production.

The following SQL syntax is the very basic DELETE statement that you can use without causing an error in your SQL engine.

DELETE FROM table;

Switch out "table" with your own table and that's all it takes to write a DELETE statement. The problem with this statement is that you essentially remove all records from the table. You have no filter in the above statement. For instance, if you replaced "table" with "Customer," you would delete all of your customer records. You obviously don't want to recover accidentally deleted data. You bring down applications and can cost a company a large sum of money in lost revenue. For this reason, you always use a filter to delete your data.

Just like the SELECT statement, you can use the WHERE clause in the DELETE statement to filter the records you remove from your tables.

**The Importance of the WHERE Clause**

Because you typically don't want to remove all of your records in any particular table, you need to add the WHERE clause to your statements. The WHERE clause in a DELETE statement is the same as the WHERE clause in the SELECT statement we worked with in the last chapter.

Let's take a look at an example.

DELETE FROM Customer WHERE customer_id = 1;

In the above statement, we only delete the customer that has an ID of 1.

You can verify that that statement only deleted your customer by using a SELECT statement. The following statement should now return no records.

SELECT * FROM Customer WHERE customer_id = 1;

The return result should look like the following.

customer_id, first_name, last_name

-----------------------------------------------------

As you can see, there are no records returned, so SQL shows you an empty data set.

In most cases, you want to delete more than one record. You need to delete a set of records. For instance, suppose you no longer support a certain product. You want to delete the product from your database. Note that there are other ways to deactivate products in a table, but we'll use this example just to give you an idea of when you would want to use the DELETE statement.

Let's see an example of a SQL statement that deletes a product named "Product A" in a Product table.

DELETE FROM Product WHERE product_name = 'Product A';

This statement deletes all records with the product named Product A. SQL should tell you the number of records affected, but it also depends on your SQL platform. You can determine if any records are deleted by using the COUNT(*) function. We'll get into this function more in subsequent chapters, but use the COUNT(*) function to determine if records are deleted if your SQL platform doesn't return the information.

Let's look at an example.

SELECT COUNT(*) FROM Product;
DELETE FROM Product WHERE product_name = 'Product A';

```
SELECT COUNT(*) FROM Product;
```

The output should look something like the following.

```
COUNT(*)
---------------------------------
5


COUNT(*)
---------------------------------
4
```

Notice that you can see the number of rows in your Product table was decremented by 1. You can safely assume that your Product table had only one product named Product A and it was successfully deleted.

You can use other operators to remove data from your tables. Suppose that you don't want log files in your database that are older than a specific date. You can use the DELETE statement with a WHERE clause filter to delete these old logs and free up disk space on your database server.

Let's take a look at an example.

```
SELECT COUNT(*) FROM Log;
DELETE FROM Log WHERE log_date >= '2001-01-01' and
log_date <= '2001-12-31';
SELECT COUNT(*) FROM Log;
```

We set up a counter to see the table row count before and after the DELETE statement to identify if any records were deleted. Notice that we used the greater than or equal to and less than or equal to operators. We haven't looked at dates in SQL yet. Notice the date format. You'll need to use the right date format when you work with MySQL.

In this example, all records in 2001 are deleted from the Log table. If any records are deleted from the table, the COUNT(*) statement lets us know since it does a count before and after the statements are run.

One common reason to use the DELETE statement is to remove duplicate records from database tables. Let's assume that you have a list of customers in an external table. These customers represent a list of duplicate customers that you want to delete from your main Customer table. You can use the EXIST clause, which is a type of operator that identifies when a record exists in another location. You can use the EXIST statement with any of the main four SQL statements. We'll show you how to use it with the DELETE statement.

Let's take a look at an example.

```
DELETE FROM Customer
WHERE EXISTS
  ( SELECT duplicates.customer_id
    FROM duplicates
);
```

In the above statement retrieves a list of customer IDs from a table named "duplicates." If the ID exists in the main Customer table, it's deleted from the main Customer table. This is just one reason that database administrators use the DELETE statement.

Of course, when you have a major deletion for a table, you should always first run the statement on a backup table or another test database that mirrors your production server. This ensures that you don't accidentally delete huge amounts of records on a production database.

## Constraints and Orphaned Records

We mentioned briefly about primary and foreign key constraints in previous chapters. The DELETE function is closely entwined with these constraints. In this section, we'll explain exactly why constraints are important for fully functional, well designed databases.

Let's assume that you have two tables named Order and Customer. You link the two tables using a foreign key that's located in the Order table. It takes some time to understand how constraints work, but think of your tables as linked spreadsheets. The customer ID is located in the Order table to link the customer to the order. You can have several orders for each customer, so you could have one or several records in the Order table with a linked customer ID.

When you set up this type of relationship, you create a primary key (the customer ID in the Customer table) and foreign key (the customer ID in the Order table) relationship. The MySQL database engine, which is our main focus, is a relational database, so it will keep data integrity intact when you create these primary-foreign key relationships.

Let's go back to the DELETE statement. What happens when you delete a customer from a table, but the customer has several orders in the Order table? You create an issue called orphaned records. You no longer have a customer associated with an order. What happens is that your application or even other database procedures expect to find a customer for each order. The result can be major bugs in your application, you can lose data, or your database procedures can't run. Multiple issues can occur, so the SQL database (as long as it's a relational database) will stop you from deleting records with a primary-foreign key relationship.

To get past the situation, you must first delete the foreign key record, and then delete the primary key record. In this example, you want to first delete the Order table records, and then delete the customer in the Customer table.

For instance, let's assume that you want to delete a customer with the ID of 1. You would first delete the records in the Order table with the same customer ID.

Let's take a look at an example.

```
SELECT COUNT(*) FROM Order;
DELETE FROM Order WHERE customer_id = 1;
SELECT COUNT(*) FROM Order;
DELETE FROM Customer WHERE customer_id = 1;
```

We only run the COUNT(*) statement on the Order table, because we expect to have several records deleted before the customer is removed. This statement ensures that we delete the order records before we delete the customer. You can highlight each statement individually in any SQL interface and run only one statement, verify the table data, and then run the second statement afterwards. If you use the MySQL command line, you can just type each statement and run after you type it.

If you didn't run the first Order table delete query, you would receive an error from the SQL engine.

### Difference Between DELETE and TRUNCATE

If you have several records to delete, the DELETE statement can reduce the performance of your database. The TRUNCATE statement lets you delete all records in your table.

This is an advantage if you have a table that you want to complete wipe. For instance, you can make backups of your current log table and want to delete the data in the current log table to free up space on the database server.

A good rule to remember is to use the DELETE statement when you want to delete several records, but you need to roll back statements or performance is not an issue. If you want to delete all of your records without the ability to roll back from database logs, you can use the TRUNCATE statement. This statement runs much faster.

The following SQL code is an example of the TRUNCATE statement.

TRUNCATE TABLE Log;

In the above statement, the SQL engine removes all records in the Log table. If you make a mistake, you must restore the data from a backup.

This chapter reviewed the DELETE function and how you can remove records from your tables. Use it wisely, but you will run across other code or the need to use the DELETE statement at some point in your career.

**Lab Questions**

1. You want to delete all records in a Log table for the year 2011. Write the SQL statement that deletes records only if they were created in 2011.
DELETE FROM Log WHERE create_date >= '2011-01-01' and log_date <= '2011-12-31';
Explanation: the above statement deletes only the records that were created in 2011.

2. If you want to delete a set of records that exist in an external table, what SQL statement do you use?

    a. IF

    b. IS NULL

    c. EXIST

    d. FOUND

Explanation: The EXIST statement lets you create a subquery that finds records in an external database to remove them.

3. You want to delete all records from the Log table. You want to do this with the best performance. Write the SQL statement.

TRUNCATE TABLE Log;

Explanation: the TRUNCATE statement is the best for performance, and it deletes all records from the table.

# Chapter 6 – Changing Data

**Chapter Objective:** At some point, the administrator needs to change or edit data in a table. This chapter covers the SQL UPDATE statement, which edits data in a table.

We've covered how to read your data and delete it, so now it's time to learn how to edit data. Editing data is just as sensitive of a task as deleting data. While data isn't completely removed from the table, you can update your data to completely inaccurate information. This leads to data integrity issues and usually a restore of your information from a backup. We'll discuss how to properly update your table's data and keep data integrity.

**The SQL UPDATE Statement**

To change your data, you use the SQL UPDATE statement. The following code is the template for updating your information.

UPDATE table SET column = 'data';

The above statement is the very basic template you use to avoid from receiving an error from bad syntax. Notice that there is no WHERE clause. We'll get into the WHERE clause in the next section, but you should know that this statement alone changes all data in your table. For instance, if the column is named "first_name" and you set the value to 'data' without the WHERE clause, all of your customer's first names are set to the value 'data.' This is a critical point to remember when designing your UPDATE statements.

Let's take a look at some better examples and put the UPDATE statement to practice. For instance, suppose your customer accidentally spelled his first name wrong. He wants to update his first name to the correctly spelled name. You would write an UPDATE statement for the application where the customer updates his information.

The following is an example of how you would change a customer's first name.

```
UPDATE Customer
SET first_name = 'john'
WHERE customer_id = 1;
```

Let's go over the above statement to better understand it. The first line is the actual UPDATE keyword, and the table's name is Customer. The Customer table must exist, or the SQL engine gives you an error.

The next line is the column you want to change. You only need to use the SET statement once when you want to change multiple column values. In this example, we are only changing the customer's first name, so we only have one column listed. The first_name column's data is set to 'john'. Even though we know that the customer spelled his name wrong, we don't care what the previous value is in the table. We change the data without checking the previous value. You can add extra checks and balances in SQL to ensure that the value is incorrect before you change it, but the UPDATE statement itself does not check for previous values when editing your table's data.

The last part of the statement is the WHERE statement. You'll recall from the previous chapters that the WHERE clause is used to filter data. Just like the DELETE statement, you need to filter the records that you edit. In this example, we only change the customer with an ID of 1. This statement assumes that the customer_id column is the primary key, so it is always unique. A primary key can never contain a duplicate value, so it's a safe way to update data without accidentally changing multiple records.

We mentioned that you can change multiple records at the same time with multiple columns. In the previous example, we used the primary key, so we know that only one record is updated. Let's assume that you need to change multiple order records. You have a product name that you've changed, and you want to change the name in the Order table.

Let's take a look at the example SQL statement.

UPDATE Order
SET product_name = 'Product B', update_date = '2015-08-21'
WHERE product_name = 'Product A';

You'll recognize that the same UPDATE statement is used in the first SQL line as we used in the previous example. This time, we're updating the Order table, so we specify the Order table name.

The next SQL line is where we specify the columns that we want to edit. In this case, we're editing the product's name and the date that we updated the record.

We haven't discussed audit fields, but most tables have a field that lets the database administrator know the last time the record was updated. In this example, our audit field is "update_date." You set these values each time you change any value in the record. We set the value to August 21, 2015. We also set the product name from Product A to Product B. We know that the previous value is Product A, because we're running our UPDATE statement's WHERE clause based on the previous product name.

To sum up this statement in words, the statement says to change a product's name to Product B where the current product's name is Product A. This is how you identify previous values in a table and only change data based on the previous value. This statement also assumes that you're changing multiple records, because you probably have more than one order with a specific product named Product A.

**Changing Your Data with External Table Data**

While there are plenty of times that you'll need to set up custom SQL statements with statically assigned values, you sometimes need to update your data from an external table. For instance, you might have a list of customers in a temporary table, and this table has more accurate information than your current customer table. You want to update the data from the external table to your current Customer table, which can be done using the SQL UPDATE statement.

To perform this query, it's a bit more advanced. Take a look at the following query.

UPDATE Customer
SET first_name = (SELECT first_name FROM temptable
WHERE Customer.customer_id = temptable.customer_id)

Notice that we didn't use a WHERE clause in the above statement. We have a temporary table named temptable that contains a list of customers that we want to update. Therefore, we only edit the customers that are contained in the temporary table.

As you can see, we have the standard UPDATE and SET statements. The difference between this statement and the previous one is that we use the first name value in the temptable to update the value in the main Customer table. This is often used when the database administrator has an external list of values that must be imported into the system. For instance, during an acquisition, the database administrator imports a number of customers from an external database.

But how does the database know which value to update from which field in the external table. Notice in the subquery that there is a WHERE clause that links the two tables. We'll get into joining tables in future chapters, but this subquery does a link between the two tables using the customer's ID. The customer_id columns in both tables presumably have the same customer IDs. When the first query pulls data from the temptable, it does a match with the customer's ID and uses the first_name column to update your Customer data.

**Updating Data from User Variables**

We discussed user variables in chapter 3. For most situations, you'll need to update your data using a user variable. The variable's value is usually sent but the application as input from your user, but sometimes database administrators work with external data that is then input as user variable values into their stored procedures.

In these examples, we'll assume that you're sending data from an application. For instance, let's go back to the previous section's example where your customer needs to update data. Since the customer isn't using static data in your SQL statements, you create a user variable that contains the input value from your customer.

Let's use the same example that we used in the first section. Let's change the query to reflect the user variable.

UPDATE Customer
SET first_name = @input
WHERE customer_id = @customerid;

We used two user variables in the above statement. The first one is named @input. Whatever value is contained in the @input variable is stored in your database. Just like the static string 'john,' if your stored procedure is sent the value of 'john' and it's stored in the user variable, the UPDATE statement changes the first_name column value to 'john'. Your application must ensure that the right information is passed to ensure that the change in data is accurate.

The next user variable is used to determine which customer you want to update. When you work with user variables and dynamic data, you pass the information you want to use to update your current tables and a user variable that defines the records you want to update. In this case, the SQL statement assumes that you're passing a customer first name and the customer ID to determine which record to change. In this case, only one record is updated, which is what you want when you change customer information.

Just like previous examples, you can also change data in multiple columns using user variables. Using the same customer example, let's update the customer's first and last name. The following SQL statement is an example of how you would perform a multi-column update.

UPDATE Customer
SET first_name = @fname, last_name = @lname
WHERE customer_id = @customerid;

In the above example, we changed the user variable names to more accurately define which user variables contain the right data. This is also important in real world situations, so you can quickly review a SQL statement and intuitively understand what data each variable contains.

This chapter gave you an overview on editing data. Just like the DELETE statement, some administrators don't allow programmers to delete data. Instead, programmers are forced to create a new record and deactivate the updated record. This is one option for properly dealing with audits and keeping a backup of any data changed.

However, at some point, you'll need to update data whether it's from an import mistake or just allowing an application to change the data in your database. This chapter gave you the fundamentals that will help you create more complex UPDATE statements.

**Lab Questions**

1. You have an application that must be able to edit a customer's last name. You want to set up a query with a user defined variable to update the customer record. Write the SQL statement that updates your customer last name using a user variable.

```
UPDATE Customer
SET last_name = @lname
WHERE customer_id = @id;
```
Explanation: the lname variable contains the customer last name, and the id variable contains the customer's ID.

2. You want to update all records with the same value in a temp table. The temp table's name is temptable and the column is temp_col. Write the UPDATE statement that updates all records.
```
UPDATE temptable
SET tem_col = 'temp';
```
Explanation: the UPDATE statement has no WHERE clause, so all records are updated with the value 'temp'.

3. You have an external table of orders that you need to import into your current database. You just want to update the product name from the external table. Write the statement that updates your current Order table with product name.
```
UPDATE Order
SET product_name = (SELECT product_name FROM temptable WHERE Order.order_id = temptable.order_id);
```
Explanation: the SQL engine updates the Order table's product_name column with the data linked in the temporary table named temptable.

# Chapter 7 – Adding Data

**Chapter Objective:** We've covered deleting, editing, and reading data from a database. This chapter covers the INSERT statement and how to add data to your database tables.

The final SQL statement that we haven't covered is the INSERT statement. This is the statement that adds new records to your database tables. For instance, when you get a new customer, you want to add a new record to your Customer table. Each time the customer orders new products, you use the INSERT statement to add a new order to your Order table. This chapter covers how you can add data to your tables using various methods and logic.

**The INSERT Statement**

The INSERT statement requires much more than the previous statements we've covered. Let's take a look at the basic template for an INSERT statement.

INSERT INTO table (column) VALUES (value);

INSERT INTO is the first part of the statement always required by the SQL engine. The "table" keyword should be changed to the table you want to work with. For instance, if you want to insert a new customer record, you need to insert into the Customer table.

The column section is used to define the columns you want to populate. You don't always need to populate all columns in a table. If you have default values and allow NULL values into your table, you can just identify the columns that are required to create a record. You separate each column with a comma in your list.

The VALUES keyword is also required with the list of values in the parenthesis. One thing to note is that the number of values must match the number of columns you list in the column list. If you don't have the same number of values as the column list, the SQL engine returns an error. Another issue to note is that you must have values in the same order as you have in the column list. If you accidentally transpose any values, you will accidentally store the wrong data in the wrong field.

Now let's take a look at an actual example. Let's insert a new customer into our Customer table.

INSERT INTO Customer (first_name, last_name) VALUES ('john', 'smith');

Notice that the above statement follows the template we posted earlier. The first and last name columns are listed in the first parenthesis with each column separated by a column. The second list is the values you want to insert. We are inserting a new customer with a first and last name of john smith. If you accidentally transposed those two values, "smith" would be inserted in the first name column and "john" would be inserted into the first name column. This is important to remember when you set values.

The above statement inserts data using static values. Notice that we didn't include the customer ID in our list of values.

The customer ID is an auto-incrementing numeric value that automatically inserts a new customer ID each time a new ID is set. This means that you don't set the customer ID. Instead, you let the database do it. This type of strategy ensures that you never have a duplicate primary key when you insert your new data. You might want to manage primary keys yourself, but some database designers make it easier to manage by simply using an auto-incrementing primary key that will never accidentally use a duplicate value. Since you always want your customers to have a unique ID, this is sometimes the better way to manage records. If you have two customers with the same ID, you could accidentally give information to the wrong customer, which can be a privacy concern.

Just like previous chapters, you probably want to insert data into your tables using user defined variables. For instance, a new customer signs up on your web page. The customer wants to send information to your database to sign up and purchase product. You do this using user defined variables sent to the application and use the INSERT statement to add the new customer record to your Customer table.

Let's take a look at an example.

INSERT INTO Customer (first_name, last_name) VALUES (@firstname, @lastname);

In the above statement, we still assume the database will automatically insert the primary key customer ID field into the table. The difference is that we used a user defined variable to insert data. If the user defined variable does not have any assigned data, the SQL engine will attempt to insert NULL into the field value. For this reason, it's best to allow NULL values into your database tables.

## Inserting Data from Another Table

We discussed updating data from a separate table in a previous chapter. You will run into times when you need to update or insert new data into your database from external sources such as external tables. The tables could come from acquisitions, or maybe you ran into a data integrity issue and need to import data from a backup table. Whatever your reason, you can use the SQL language to pretty easily import data into your database without creating and running complex SQL statements.

Let's use the same example as the Customer table example from the previous chapter. Instead of updating data, you want to insert new records into your database. You have an external temporary table named temptable. You want to import the customers listed in the temptable. We'll also assume that the temptable has the same structure as the Customer table since this course is for beginners.

Let's take a look at an example.

INSERT INTO Customer (first_name, last_name)
SELECT first_name, last_name FROM temptable;

Notice that we didn't use the VALUES keyword. We don't use it when you pull data from an external table. Instead, we just use a SELECT statement to pull records from the external temporary table. In this example, we extract every record in the table and insert it into the Customer table. Notice that the columns are the same as the columns in the main Customer table.

You also have the option to filter the records that you want to import.

For instance, suppose you only want to import customers in the temporary table that were created at a specific date. You can add the WHERE clause to your SELECT query to filter the records that are inserted into your table.

Let's take a look at an example.

INSERT INTO Customer (first_name, last_name)
SELECT first_name, last_name FROM temptable
WHERE create_date >= '2012-08-31';

In the above example, only customer records created after August 31, 2012 are inserted into your Customer table. This is useful when you have several records that you don't need inserted into your tables. It's a way to take a large data dump and still use it to transform your data from one table to another.

What happens when you just want to take a snapshot of a temporary table with several columns? For instance, you could have a table of customers and the table contains dozens of columns. While this isn't a very well designed table, it can happen when you have a CSV file that you've recently imported into your database.

If you want to just create a copy of your database and don't want to specify columns the target and source tables must be exactly the same. Any changes in the column structure and the database won't understand how to import the tables and match the different columns.

Let's take a look at an example in the following SQL statement.

INSERT INTO Customer
SELECT first_name, last_name FROM temptable;

In the above example, notice that there are not columns specified, but the columns are the same in the temporary table as they are in the target table. This allows the SQL database to match up the appropriate column for both the source and the destination.

**Autoincrementing Fields and Default Values**

In most cases, you won't insert all data columns into your database tables when you use an INSERT statement. You use default values to automatically set the field value, so you don't need to specify it each time. For instance, your customer could enter a first and last name, but you might want to allow the customer to enter their address at another time. When the customer signs up on your website, you don't capture the address information, so you have no value for the address field in your table. You do this using default values. A default value is set when you design your tables.

If you recall, we discussed how to create tables. The NOT NULL specification was used for primary keys, because these keys can't contain NULL values. However, we specified NULL for other columns.

Let's do a select statement on the information we just entered into our Customer table. We didn't specify an address, so what happens to the column when we specify just the first and last name?

SELECT * FROM Customer;

The output should look like the following.

customer_id, first_name, last_name, address
---------------------------------------------------------------------
1      Jane    Jones  NULL

2      John   Smith  NULL

Notice our new John Smith record that we created. The address is set to NULL. This is because we did not specify a value and we allowed NULL values in our address column. If you didn't allow NULL values, the SQL engine would return an error.

Also notice that the customer has an ID even though we didn't manually set one. This is because our Customer table is set up to automatically take the last record in the database table, increment it by 1, and then insert the new value into the Customer table record. We know that each record inserted with have a unique ID.

This chapter covered the basics of inserting new records into your tables. The INSERT statement is probably the second most common statement that you'll write after the SELECT statement.

**Lab Questions**

1. You need to insert a record into your Order table. The table has two columns named product_name and total_order_cost. Write the SQL statement that inserts a new record into the Order table.

INSERT INTO Order (product_name, total_order_cost) VALUES ('Product Name', 10.00);

Explanation: We used the simple INSERT statement to add the record. Notice that numeric values are not enclosed by tick marks.

2. You want to insert a new customer record into your Customer table. You want to use user defined variables. Write the SQL statement that inserts a new record. Assume the Customer table has two columns named first_name and last_name.

INSERT INTO Customer (first_name, last_name) VALUES (@firstname, @lastname);

Explanation: Instead of using static values, the user defined variables are used to insert data.

3. What is the name of a field that you can use for primary keys to ensure that each field has a unique value?

    a. NULL
    b. NULL values
    c. Integer
    d. Autoincrement

Explanation: An autoincrement field increments the last number from a previous record to ensure that you always get a unique value for your primary keys.

# Chapter 8 – Joining Tables

**Chapter Objective:** It's not enough to just read data from 1 table. Most applications require data from multiple relational tables. This chapter explains how to use the JOIN statement to select from multiple linked tables.

We covered the SELECT statement in previous chapters. You use the SELECT statement to read data from your tables. We also covered primary and foreign key relationships. You need these relationships to link tables. This chapter will help you understand how to join tables on primary and foreign keys to create larger, more complex data sets. Joining two tables together is much more efficient than reading multiple tables separately, and you'll find that you join your tables much more frequently than just querying one table in a relational database.

## An Overview of Joining Tables

In previous chapters, we used several different SELECT statements to review data from a table. Let's use the same example of customers and orders. You have two tables that list your customers, and for each customer one or more records could exist in the orders table. You could do a select on the Customer table and get a customer ID, and then you could do a second SELECT statement on the Order table and get a list of orders. As you can imagine, if you must do this with several tables, it can greatly reduce the performance of your applications.

This is where a JOIN statement comes in handy. The JOIN statement lets you combined the results of the customer and orders and display one data set result. This not only gives you one data set for all queries, but it also reduces the amount of queries on the database server. When you have thousands of people using your database, poorly optimized queries and stored procedures result in sluggishness of your database server and your application. This costs companies money, so your goal as a database programmer or administrator is to make your SQL statements as efficient as possible.

**The Inner Join Statement**

The first JOIN statement you need to know is the INNER JOIN. There is some logic and understanding you have to know before you start running join statements. An INNER JOIN basically says "join these two tables together and only give me records that have a match in both tables." For instance, if you have a customer with no orders, an INNER JOIN statement excludes the customer because there is no match between the two tables. With this type of join statement, you have no null records with unmatched links.

Let's take a look at an example using the Customer and Order tables.

SELECT c.first_name, c.last_name, o.order_id,
o.product_name
FROM Customer AS c
INNER JOIN Order AS o ON c.customer_id = o.customer_id
WHERE c.customer_id = 1;

You'll notice that this statement is much longer and more complex than previous SELECT statements we've used. Let's dissect the statement and review it further.

The fist line is the standard SELECT syntax that defines that we want to read data and return the customer's first and last name. We also return some order information to review the customer's list of orders.

The next line defines the first table we're querying. We added the AS statement. The AS statement lets us create aliases for tables. Aliases are shorthand notations for specific tables. Once you define the alias, you must use it throughout your SQL statements. Aliases make it easier to type long SQL statements, and they make shorter statements that are easier to read when an administrator reviews the code.

The third line of code is the INNER JOIN statement. We're joining on the customer_id column, which as we mentioned before is the primary and foreign key relationship. The customer_id column should be unique for the Customer table, but it could be used in multiple records in the Order table. For this reason, if you have multiple orders in the Order table, the data set returns the customer information for each Order, so it looks like duplicate records. When you review the data, just remember that the data set does not represent the number of times the record is in the table.

Let's assume that there are two orders in the Order table for customer ID 1. Let's take a look at what the record set looks like.

first_name, last_name, order_id, product_name
---------------------------------------------------------------------------

John   smith  1      Product A
John   smith  2      Product B

Notice that the customer's name is listed twice. That's because the records returned are for two orders for the same customer. The order_id and the product name are both different. This indicates that there are two orders in your Order table.

What happens if there are no orders in the Order table? No records are returned. As a matter of fact, you get a completely empty data set even though the customer does exist in the Customer table. The INNER JOIN statement only returns records where both tables have records for a specific relationship.

When you work with the JOIN statement, you have to remember these SQL quirks to ensure that you receive an accurate data set. When you only have a few records to work with, it's easy to do a quick review of the information and determine if you've worked with the right JOIN statement and logic. However, when you work with thousands of records, you might accidentally retrieve and work with the wrong data. If you join on the wrong relationship, use the wrong WHERE filter clause or use the wrong alias in your statements, you can create a data set that returns the wrong information. This is mostly important when you work with reports that require accuracy but you're unable to review data before it's published publicly.

**The LEFT JOIN Statement**

We worked with a data set that returned only data for customers with orders, but what if you want a list of customers and then any connecting orders.
What if you want to review a customer even if they don't have an order? The INNER JOIN statement removes customers with no orders, but you have the option of working with the LEFT JOIN statement.

The LEFT JOIN statement basically states "give me all records from the left table and any records that match on the right table." Think of the Customer table as the left table, and the Order table as the right table.

The LEFT JOIN statement often gives you a larger record set, so you don't want to use it if you don't need it. It's better to use the INNER JOIN statement when you don't need all records from one table, because large record sets can slow the database and your application.

Let's take a look at an example query using the same Customer and Order tables we previously used for the INNER JOIN query.

```
SELECT c.first_name, c.last_name, o.order_id,
o.product_name
FROM Customer AS c
LEFT JOIN Order AS o ON c.customer_id = o.customer_id
WHERE c.customer_id = 1;
```

Notice that we used the exact same query except we traded the INNER JOIN for a LEFT JOIN. We still use aliases and we still query for only orders that exist for customer ID 1. Let's assume, though, that customer 1 has no orders. If you recall, we said that with an INNER JOIN, the data set would be empty. Let's see what happens with a LEFT JOIN.

Here is an example of our data output.

first_name, last_name, order_id, product_name
----------------------------------------------------------------------------
John    smith  NULL NULL

Notice that we don't have an empty data set, but the order information returned is NULL. The data set also contains only one record. We have only one customer with an ID of 1, so only one record is returned, but we have no order records. Unlike the INNER JOIN statement, the LEFT JOIN statement returns all records from the left table (Customer) and displays NULL if no records exist on the right table (Orders). If you had orders for the customer, the record set would return the same list as the INNER JOIN query.

This is a distinct difference, and as you can guess, just changing to the wrong type of JOIN statement greatly influences the records you return. If we needed a report that listed all customers with any of their orders and used the INNER JOIN statement, the report would have the wrong number of customers. With the LEFT JOIN statement, we get the right number of customers with any orders associated with the customer.

**The RIGHT JOIN Statement**

The RIGHT JOIN statement is similar to the LEFT JOIN. The only difference is that the RIGHT JOIN statement says "give me all records on the right table and any matches on the left table." In our example, instead of taking all records from the Customer table, the SQL engine is instructed to take all records from the right table (Orders) and return any results. Since every order needs a customer, you would get a record for each order that you retrieve. However, this would be a good way to determine if you have orphaned records on a table that doesn't have the proper constraints.

Let's take a look at an example using the same query to give us an understanding of the data results.

```
SELECT c.first_name, c.last_name, o.order_id,
o.product_name
FROM Customer AS c
RIGHT JOIN Order AS o ON c.customer_id = o.customer_id
WHERE c.customer_id = 1;
```

Again, we've only changed the JOIN statement and nothing else. Let's take a look at the data results.

first_name, last_name, order_id, product_name

----------------------------------------------------------------------------

John    smith  1        Product A
John    smith  2        Product B

Notice that our result set is the same as the INNER JOIN. Let's take away the WHERE clause filter and look at the data set again.

Here is the query.

```
SELECT c.first_name, c.last_name, o.order_id,
o.product_name
FROM Customer AS c
RIGHT JOIN Order AS o ON c.customer_id = o.customer_id
```

Let's take a look at the results.

first_name, last_name, order_id, product_name

----------------------------------------------------------------------------

John    smith  1        Product A
John    smith  2        Product B
NULL NULL 3             Product A

Notice we have all records from the Order table, but there is a NULL value for the customer information for order 3. Since we're supposed to have a constraint, it looks like we forgot to restrict deletion of a customer if the customer has an order. The result is that we have an order with no customer linked to it, and this is what we use the RIGHT JOIN statement for.

These are the main three JOIN statements you'll need to know when you work with multiple relational tables. It takes some practice to get used to the right results, so let's look at some lab questions.

## Lab Questions

1. You need to query for all of your customers and orders. You want to get a count of all customers and any related orders even if they don't have one. Write the SQL query that accomplishes this.
SELECT c.first_name, c.last_name, o.order_id, o.product_name
FROM Customer AS c
LEFT JOIN Order AS o ON c.customer_id = o.customer_id;
Explanation: You use the LEFT JOIN to get all customers on the left table and then join to the right table, which is the Order table.

2. You want to query customers with an order. You want to filter out any customers that don't have an order. Write the SQL statement that gets this data set.
SELECT c.first_name, c.last_name, o.order_id, o.product_name
FROM Customer AS c
INNER JOIN Order AS o ON c.customer_id = o.customer_id
Explanation: the INNER JOIN statement filters out any records where there is not a match.

3. What SQL keyword is used to create an alias for a table name in your queries?

    a. ALIAS

    b. AS

    c. AT

    d. ALSO

Explanation: The AS keyword lets you create shorthand names for your table names as you query them.

# Chapter 9 – Aggregating Data

**Chapter Objective:** SQL has several functions that let you automatically aggregate, average, or add up values in your tables. This chapter covers the main SQL functions for working with large sets of data.

SQL lets you automate several common math commands. For instance, if you want to see the total amount of sales for the day, you can use the internal SQL function named SUM. You can also average, count, and identify maximum and minimum values. There are several internal functions that help reduce programming time and effort and do the procedure for you. This chapter covers these main functions to make your SQL programming life easier.

**The COUNT Function**

We'll start off with the easiest of all the aggregate functions. The COUNT function simply counts the number of records returned. For instance, maybe you just want a count of the total customers in your Customer table to give you an idea of the number of customers you've acquired. Maybe you want to get a count of orders between certain dates to identify the number of orders you've received. Both of these examples use the COUNT function.

Let's take a look at an example.

SELECT COUNT(*) FROM Customer;

The above statement counts all records in your customer table. You might have duplicate records, but you can get a general idea of the number of customers you've acquired from your website or application.

Maybe you want to get a list of customers that signed up at a certain time. This would require the WHERE clause. Instead of counting all records in a table, using the WHERE clause will give you a count of the number of customers who signed up at a specific date. Let's look at an example.

SELECT COUNT(*) FROM Customer
WHERE create_date >= '2015-08-01' and create_date <= '2015-08-31';

As you can see, the query only returns a count for customers who signed up in August 2015. This too is useful when you want to see the progression of your website or business. This type of query is often used in reporting.

**The SUM Function**

The SUM function is the answer to any aggregation that you need to sum. For instance, suppose you need to add up all order totals for a specific date. You could take each record one by one and add up the results, but you can use the SUM function instead. The SUM function lets you add up totals and makes it easy to get these values. One note about the SUM function is that it ignores NULL values. Any NULL values are ignored, so you can view a NULL value as 0 although it only works with this function and not others.

Let's take a look at an example.

SELECT SUM(order_total) FROM Order

WHERE create_date >= '2015-08-01' and create_date <= '2015-08-31';

The SUM function adds up all order_total values between the two dates indicated and provides you with the output.

Suppose you want to SUM up values for each specific customer. This introduces the necessity of the GROUP BY clause. This clause groups records by the specified field, so you can get output for a specific group.

Let's take a look at an example.

SELECT SUM(order_total) AS total, customer_id FROM Order
WHERE create_date >= '2015-08-01' and create_date <= '2015-08-31'
GROUP BY customer_id;

We added some statements to the SQL code. We gave an alias to the total, so we can more easily identify the column that contains the summed data. We then specify the customer_id column. We want to group a total amount by the customer_id field, so we then have the amount a customer spent for each customer ID.

Let's take a look at the output for the above query.

total, customer_id
-------------------------------------------------
44.00   1
43.00   2

The above output gives you the totals for customers 1 and 2. You can combine this statement with the COUNT statement to also identify the number of orders. For instance, you know that customer 1 had a total of 44.00 in order costs, but how many orders is that? You don't know the number of orders that make up the $44.00. Let's combine the COUNT function with the SUM function to identify the number of orders.

SELECT SUM(order_total) AS total, COUNT(order_total) AS order_count, customer_id FROM Order
WHERE create_date >= '2015-08-01' and create_date <= '2015-08-31'
GROUP BY customer_id;

Now let's take a look at the results.

```
total, order_count, customer_id
-------------------------------------------------
44.00  2      1
43.00  3      2
```

Now we have a more accurate report. We know that customer 1 made two orders that total up to $44.00. You've just written your first basic report that could be useful for the website owner. Remember that whenever you need to group data, which is common when you need to do aggregating functions, you always need to use the GROUP BY statement.

**The AVG Function**

The AVG function is a bit trickier than the SUM function. The AVG does as the name suggests – it averages a group of records.

However, when you could identify an ignored NULL value as a 0, which the AVG function the record is ignored. This means that if your record set has 4 records but one has a NULL value, the AVG function adds up only 3 records and uses that 3 records as the averaging denominator in the calculation.

Let's take a look at the AVG function SQL sample.

SELECT AVG(order_total) AS total, customer_id FROM Order
WHERE create_date >= '2015-08-01' and create_date <= '2015-08-31'
GROUP BY customer_id;

We again group our data using the customer ID. We use the same query except for the AVG function. Let's take a look at the sample data.

```
total, customer_id
-------------------------------------------------
12.00          1
13.00          2
```

Now we have the average amount spent from each of your customers. But what if you want to include values that are NULL? You need to turn the NULL value to a 0 for the query. We can use the IFNULL function. The IFNULL function changes a value when it's NULL. It's not changed permanently in your tables. Instead, the IFNULL function changes the value just for the query. Therefore, if we need to know the average of customer orders even if the customer spent no money, we include the IFNULL function.

Let's take a look at an example.

```
SELECT AVG(IFNULL(order_total, 0)) AS total, customer_id
FROM Order
WHERE create_date >= '2015-08-01' and create_date <= '2015-
08-31'
GROUP BY customer_id;
```

Now we have the IFNULL included to switch a NULL value to 0 for the calculation. Now the SQL statement will have a more accurate average. Let's take a look at the results and its changes.

```
total, customer_id
------------------------------------------------
4.00          1
13.00         2
```

Since our average went down for customer ID 1, we know that this customer has some orders with a 0 sum total. This is beneficial when you have several records that average in your queries, but you can't identify which ones return NULL values. Now you know that you have NULL values in your data set.

**The MIN and MAX Functions**

The final two aggregate functions that you need to know are the MIN and MAX functions. These two functions find the highest and lowest values in a data set. For instance, you might want to know your biggest order for the month, or maybe you just want to know the last customer ID that was entered into your database. Maybe you want to know the smallest order amount as well. All of these values can be found using the MIN and MAX functions.

Let's use the same query we've been using. We want to know the total of all orders for the month of August, be we also want to know the maximum order value within the record set.

Take a look at the following SQL statement.

SELECT SUM(order_total, 0) AS total, MAX(order_total) as max, customer_id FROM Order
WHERE create_date >= '2015-08-01' and create_date <= '2015-08-31'
GROUP BY customer_id;

Notice that we removed the AVG function and replaced it with the SUM function. We want to know the summation of all of our orders, so we want to use the SUM function. We added the MAX function. This function will tell us what the maximum order is for each customer. And finally, remember that we always need the GROUP BY statement to ensure that the SQL database doesn't return an error to our output and it properly groups each total by the customer ID.

Now let's take a look at the output. The following data set is returned from our MySQL database.

total, max, customer_id
-----------------------------------------------
44.00  10     1
13.00  11     2

Now we know the maximum order total for each customer. Customer 1 had a maximum order of 10 and a total of 44.00, and customer 2 had a maximum order total of 11 with a total of 13.

Now let's do the opposite. Suppose you want to know the smallest order in a customer's order history. You use the MIN function to find the smallest value in a grouped set. Let's take a look at an example.

SELECT SUM(order_total, 0) AS total, MIN(order_total) as min, customer_id FROM Order
WHERE create_date >= '2015-08-01' and create_date <= '2015-08-31'
GROUP BY customer_id;

Notice that we have the same SELECT statement. The only difference between this statement and the previous one is the use of the MIN function. Now we're finding the smallest order total for each customer.

Let's take a look at an example of the data set returned by SQL.

```
total, min, customer_id
-------------------------------------------------
44.00  4      1
13.00  3      2
```

Now we know that customer 1 has a minimum order total of 4, and customer 2 has a minimum order value of 3. From the totaled values, we know that these orders aren't the only orders for the customer, so we can assume that each of these customers has more than one order. If the minimum or maximum returned values were the same as the total value, then the customer could presumably only have one order. This is the type of extrapolation you'll need to make when you review data sets from your SQL queries.

That's it! Those are the main aggregate functions in SQL. SQL has several different internal functions, but these are the most common for database administrators and programmers. Let's take a look at some lab questions for you to write some statements on your own.

## Lab Questions

1. You want to get the total order for all records created in August. You don't want to group them. You just want the total number of orders for a gross revenue estimate. Write the SQL query that gives you the right value.
SELECT SUM(order_total) FROM Order
WHERE create_date >= '2015-08-01' and create_date <= '2015-08-31';
Explanation: this query sums up all records for the month of August.

2. What statement must you use if you want to group records?
    a. ORDER BY
    b. FILTER BY
    c. GROUP BY
    d. TOTAL
Explanation: the GROUP BY function should be added to the end of any SQL statement that requires grouping by a specific field.

3. You want to get an average for each customer in your Order table. Write the query that gets an average order total for each customer for the month of August.
SELECT AVG(order_total) AS total, customer_id FROM Order
WHERE create_date >= '2015-08-01' and create_date <= '2015-08-31'
GROUP BY customer_id;

Explanation: Remember that the average function removes and disregards any records with NULL values.

# Chapter 10 – Subqueries

**Chapter Objective:** Subqueries are SELECT statements used to refine a filtered list of results. You use subqueries to query a separate table for a list of results included within your main query. The objective for this chapter is to write subqueries for our SELECT statements.

We had one small example of a subquery in the previous chapter that covered the UPDATE statement. This chapter is dedicated to SQL subqueries, which are usually implemented in SELECT statements. They are sometimes considered more advanced programming techniques in SQL, but it's important to understand how they work as you'll probably find yourself working with them in most applications, even if you do minimal SQL programming on the database side.

Subqueries are basically a "query within a query." They query a secondary table, return results, and then your outer, main query retrieves results from the subquery. The subquery can be used as filter in the WHERE clause or a way to retrieve a field from a secondary table in the list of columns you want to retrieve.

One thing to note with a subquery is that they are not an efficient way to query database results. Most database administrators require developers to change any subqueries into more efficient table joins, which we covered in the previous chapter. There are some rare occasions that you still need to use them, which is why we are covering them in this ebook.

## Sub SELECT Queries

We covered a sub SELECT query in a previous chapter with an UPDATE statement. The UPDATE statement changed the values of specific columns with a value returned from a sub SELECT query. A sub SELECT query can be used in any of the four main statements that we've covered. We'll focus mostly on SELECT statements, because they are easier to test without accidentally destroying your data.

Let's take a look at an example query that uses a sub SELECT statement.

```
SELECT first_name, last_name,
(SELECT order_id FROM Order where Order.customer_id =
c.customer_id LIMIT 1) AS orderid
FROM Customer AS c
WHERE c.customer_id = 1;
```

While the above query isn't the most efficient compared to a query that uses the JOIN statement, it's sometimes used in more complex statements. We're using this query to help you understand subqueries without diving into more complex statements that could be too difficult for a beginner to understand.

Let's dissect the above query to help you understand how it works. The first line of code is the typical SELECT statement with the first and last name defined as the columns we want to review. The next line of code is the subquery that you might recognize. The subquery retrieves an order that matches the customer's ID number. You'll notice that we had to prefix the column filters in the subquery. Without doing this, the SQL engine doesn't know which customer_id column to use – the main query or the subquery.

With this definition, we know that the MySQL database engine will use the customer_id column from the right tables as we've defined them.

You'll notice a new SQL statement added to the subquery. LIMIT is the SQL keyword used to define the number of records returned from a query. You can use the LIMIT statement in both the main query and the subquery. The LIMIT statement in this subquery is important or the SQL engine will return an error to your program. The reason SQL returns an error is because you could possibly have several orders that match a customer ID. If you can visualize it, multiple returned orders would produce multiple results for one record in your main query. This creates a problem for SQL and returns an error. Therefore, whenever you use subqueries in this type of way, you should always limit the returned value to 1 to avoid errors from your SQL engine.

We also alias the subquery. When a value is returned from the subquery, if we don't set a subquery alias, SQL picks a default for us. We want to know exactly what column is returned, so we set the subquery alias as orderid to make the data set results clearer.

The next part of the main query should be familiar to you. It determines that you want to return records from the Customer table, and we set an alias named c for the table. This c alias is used in the subquery to ensure that the SQL engine knows to query from the right table using the appropriate column.

Let's take a look at the example data set returned from the above query.

first_name, last_name, orderid
----------------------------------------------------------

John   Smith        1

In the above sample record set, you'll see that we get similar results as we received in previous chapters that discussed joining our tables together. The customer with the name John Smith is associated with the order ID of 1. The subquery used the associated link to return the right value for John's order.

Another issue to note when you use subquery values. Always remember that the inner subquery runs first, and then the main query runs. This means that if your subquery returns a million records but the main outer query only returns a few records, the procedure is actually very inefficient. This can slow down your database performance. Remember to keep your subqueries to a minimum in your database code to avoid this type of pitfall where subqueries return too many records.

**The IN Statement**

The IN statement is a common way to use subqueries to filter a main query results using the WHERE clause filters. As you know, the WHERE clause filters a main query's result. You can use a subquery in your WHERE clause to filter out results returned from an external table.

Let's take a look at a sample query with a subquery to identify how the IN statement works. We'll use our standard Order and Customer table as an example, but most queries that use subqueries can be more complex.

Here is an example query.

```
SELECT first_name, last_name
FROM Customer AS c
WHERE c.customer_id = 1
And
```

c.customer_id in (SELECT customer_id FROM Order);

Notice that we moved the subquery from the main part of the statement and changed it a little bit. The subquery no longer links the Customer table and it has no limit. The way this query returns results is to first query all customer IDs from the Order table. Then, the main query runs. If the customer ID is found in the Order table, then the customer is returned.

Let's take a look at the results.

first_name, last_name
-----------------------------------------------------------
John    Smith
Jane    Smith

We have two records displayed in the record set. This tells us that both John and Jane have orders in the Order table, because the IN statement only displays records that were actually found in the subquery table.

Again note that all records in the subquery are returned first and then the main query is executed. If you have a million records in the Order table, this means that the database would first have to process results for a million records, then use the main query to filter these millions of records. This is an inefficient use of database resources. A better way to query this table would be to use a JOIN statement to JOIN tables and then use the WHERE clause to filter results. You will, however, run into this type of querying when you work with other people's SQL code.

You'll also note that we didn't use the LIMIT function with this subquery.

That's because we need to return all customer ID records from the Order table to allow the main query to find each customer ID in the list. Since we don't want just one record but all order records that contain a customer ID should be used to match all customers with all orders.

**The NOT IN Statement**

We used the IN statement in the previous section. We used a subquery to find records that are in a separate table. With the NOT IN statement, we can find a list of records in a table and exclude them from the main query. While the previous section displayed a list of customers that were in the Order table, we now want to exclude any customer that is in the Order table. You would do this, for instance, if you wanted to find all customers that do not have an order. If the customer is in the Order table, you know that the customer has an order. If the customer ID is not in the Order table, the customer doesn't have an order. Since the NOT IN statement is used to find IDs that are not in the Order table, this is a way to find these customers.

Let's take a look at an example.

SELECT first_name, last_name
FROM Customer AS c
WHERE c.customer_id = 1
And
c.customer_id NOT IN (SELECT customer_id FROM Order);

Notice that the query is exactly the same as the previous query that used the IN statement. The difference with this new query is that we use the NOT IN statement instead of just IN. The NOT IN logic is exactly the opposite as the IN statement.

Let's take a look at the results for the above query.

first_name, last_name
--------------------------------------------------------

Notice that we have a completely empty data set. Since the logic is exactly the opposite, we know that the results should be exactly the opposite when we run the statement. The query basically says "give me all records in the Customer table that are not found in the Order table." Since we found both of our customers in the first statement, we know that both of our customers have orders. The NOT IN statement only displays a customer if the ID is NOT found in the Order table. Therefore, the database returns no records since the customer was indeed found in the Order table.

That's all there is to a subquery. You won't see them too much in the database administration and programming world, but you will run into them as you work on more complex queries from other coders. Remember to use JOIN statements when you can instead of subqueries, and test your statements to ensure that each query is optimized before you upload and deploy inefficient queries that take too many resources on your database server.

## Lab Questions

1. You want to return all customers that are found in the Customer table. You want to use the IN statement to find customer IDs in the Order table and found in the Customer table to identify customers with an order. Write the SQL statement to do this.

SELECT first_name, last_name
FROM Order AS o
WHERE o.customer_id = 1
And
o.customer_id in (SELECT customer_id FROM Customer);

Explanation: This statement is a bit different than the chapter's example. This statement gets all customers in the Order table and gets any customers in the Customer table to identify if your customer has an order.

2. What should you use with a subquery that is used to return a column in your main query?

    a. LIMIT
    b. ADD
    c. SUM
    d. TOP

Explanation: The LIMIT statement returns a set number of records from a subquery.

3. Take the SQL query you wrote for the first lab question and reverse its logic. Write the query that finds customers that don't have an order.

SELECT first_name, last_name
FROM Order AS o
WHERE o.customer_id = 1
And
o.customer_id NOT IN (SELECT customer_id FROM Customer);

Explanation: the NOT IN statement reverses your logic when you use the IN statement.

# Chapter 11 – Cursors and Views

**Chapter Objective:** Cursors are the SQL versions of loops in programming. Views are used to build a virtual table from a pre-defined query. This chapter's objective is to help you understand how to work with cursor loops and view objects.

If you're familiar with any type of programming language, you'll understand the loop concept. A loop is a block of code that continuously runs the same commands until a certain condition is met. The condition is your choice as long as the logic is right. If you have incorrect logic in your code, you can create what is called an infinite loop.

We'll also discuss views. Views are predefined result sets that come from a query. The difference between a view and a regular query is that a view can't have dynamic values. For instance, if you want to perform queries on a list of orders from a specific date, you would define those dates and then use the view in the same way you'd use a table.

We'll discuss both of these concepts in the next sections.

## Cursors

Cursors are a bit more advanced than standard SQL queries. We've discussed several concepts that you will run into any time you work with SQL.
Cursors can put a huge strain on server resources, so they are generally avoided by database administrators.

This doesn't mean that they are never used, but they are used sparingly to avoid any resource intensive activity that could otherwise reduce performance on the server.

There are some times that you won't be able to avoid using a cursor. You might also need to identify performance issues with other coder cursors. For this reason, it's important to understand how cursors work, and you should know how to script one yourself.

A cursor takes several lines of SQL code. Let's take each SQL statement line by line, so we can explain how they work.

Let's take a look at the first statement for a cursor.

```
DECLARE mycursor CURSOR FOR
SELECT customer_id FROM Order;
```

You'll recognize the DECLARE statement. This statement declares the cursor within the SQL database and tells the database server to allocate resources for it. Cursors take huge amounts of memory to process if the data set is large, so this is why you must remember to use cursors only if it's necessary.

The CURSOR FOR statement leads into the SELECT statement. Every cursor must be associated with a SELECT statement. Think of the SELECT statement as a way to load the cursor with the necessary values it needs to loop through records. As you can see, we retrieve all customer ID fields from the Order table. We only have a couple of records in the Order table, but if this was an active table, you could have millions of records. Imagine the memory needed to keep track of millions of records? This is why you must optimize your cursors with the right memory management.

The final point in the previous statement is to take note of the cursor name, because we'll need it as we loop through cursor records. In this example, we named the cursor mycursor.

Here is the next line of cursor code for our database.

OPEN mycursor;

The above statement is short, but it's important. This statement tells the SQL database engine to open the cursor and load the records from the SELECT statement.

Now we need to fetch the records and place them into variables. Take a look at the following line of code.

FETCH mycursor INTO mycustomerid;

Again, this statement is short, but it's an important part of the cursor process. We specify that we want to fetch records from the cursor named mycursor. We then place these records into a list of variables. Because we only retrieved records with one column each, we only need to use one variable. However, if we had several returned columns from the SELECT statement, we'd need to create a list of variables each separated by a comma. In other words, for each column in your SELECT statement, you must have a custom variable used in the FETCH statement.

Once you have these three statements set up, you can now use your own custom logic and SQL code to manipulate and work with the data.

Just as an example, let's just print the customer's name.

We have the customer ID from the Order table, so we need to create a user variable and use it to contain each customer name as we loop through records. Here's an example of how we can do this.

```
SET@customer = NULL;
SELECT @customer := first_name FROM Customer WHERE customer_id = mycustomerid;
SELECT @customer;
```

This statement is similar to what we covered in chapter 3. A user variable named @customer is created. We then use this variable to contain the customer's first name. The mycustomerid variable set in our FETCH statement contains the value for each customer ID each time you loop. This block of code just retrieves the customer's first name and prints the output to the SQL console. In most instances, you'll want to manipulate values and return the results to an application or insert the data into your tables.

After you are finished looping through your list of values, you need to close the cursor. The following statement closes your cursor and frees up resources.

```
CLOSE mycursor;
```

You can also declare an error handler for cursors. For instance, suppose you skip records and your loop ends unexpectedly early. When this happens, your SQL database engine returns an error. To avoid the issue, you just need to add the following line of code to your program.

```
DECLARE CONTINUE HANDLER FOR NOT FOUND SET finished = 1;
```

That's it! If your cursor runs into an issue, it aborts and continues with the rest of your statements.

This example was a simple cursor, but you can get much more complex and work with much more advanced logic within cursors, which is another reason most database administrators prefer for them to be avoided.

**Views**

Now that you understand cursors, you can move on to views. Views are much different than cursors, but they also provide a way for you to work with large sets of data that are otherwise too complex for a simple SELECT statement.

Views have a different logic behind why you want to use them. For instance, suppose your application frequently retrieves a list of customers and any related orders. Every time you write a SQL procedure, you have to recreate the SELECT statement that performs the join between the two statements. Each time SQL needs to run this statement, it uses memory and CPU resources. You want to optimize and streamline your SQL code, which you can do if you implement a view.

A view takes the place of frequently used stored procedures or SQL statements. Let's use the example of our customers and orders that we've used throughout this ebook. We continuously perform searches for customers and their related orders. Let's take a look at the query.

SELECT c.first_name, c.last_name, o.order_id
FROM Customer AS c
JOIN Order AS o on c.customer_id = o.customer_id;

We didn't add a WHERE clause to the statement, because we can't add dynamic values to the SELECT statement for a view. We just need a full list of values returned from the SELECT query, and then we can work to filter these values once we create the view.

The above statement queries the database for a list of customers and orders, but it's not a view. Let's use the query to create a view. The code to do this is below.

```
CREATE VIEW Customer_Orders AS
SELECT c.first_name, c.last_name, o.order_id
FROM Customer AS c
JOIN Order AS o on c.customer_id = o.customer_id;
```

You'll notice that we have the same SELECT query we used earlier. The difference is that we added the CREATE VIEW to the beginning of the statement. We then gave the view a name. The name should describe the view. In this case, we have a view that gives us the customer's information and orders, so we name it Customer_Orders.

With the view created, you can use it in the same way you use a table. Let's take a look at an example.

```
SELECT * FROM Customer_Orders;
```

The results look like the following data set.

```
first_name, last_name, order_id
------------------------------------------------------------
John    Smith 1
Jane    Smith 2
```

From our previous examples, we know that this is all customers with an order. What if we only want one customer? We can use the view just like a table, so we can use the WHERE clause with the query we used previously. Let's take a look at an example.

```
SELECT * FROM Customer_Orders
WHERE customer_id = 1;
```

Now the data set returned is the following.

```
first_name, last_name, order_id
-----------------------------------------------------------
John   Smith 1
```

With the data set above, we know that a customer with the ID of 1 is John Smith. John has 1 order with an ID of 1.

You can use views in all the same ways as you use a table. You can join records, perform complex SELECT statements, and you can even use them in your cursors.

There is one thing you can't do with a view. You can't update records in a view like you can with a regular query. For instance, if you return a list of customer records and you want to manually change values in your SQL interface, you won't be able to change them. You'll need to run your changes on the actual data instead of the view. Remember views are a virtual table that represents a list of data queries that you use often.

Once you get some practice with views and cursors, you'll be able to write them without reference. Just remember that both views and cursors are related to SELECT statements.

You need to identify the data you need to consolidate in both cases and use that statement to load both objects. This is sometimes the hard part when you need to manage data across several tables.


**Lab Questions**

1. You want to create a cursor that retrieves a list of customers. Write the first two SQL statements needed to create the cursor.
DECLARE mycursor CURSOR FOR
SELECT customer_id FROM Customer;
OPEN CURSOR mycursor;
Explanation: The first statement declares the cursor and names it mycursor. The next statement actually opens the cursor for use in your loop.

2. Using the above example, write the next SQL statement that defines variables for the cursor.
FETCH mycursor INTO mycustomerid;
Explanation: the FETCH statement gets a list of columns and assigns each column a variable in the INTO section of the statement.

3. You want to create a view that lists all customers and their associated orders. Write the SQL statement that accomplishes this.
CREATE VIEW Customer_Orders AS
SELECT c.first_name, c.last_name, o.order_id
FROM Customer AS c
JOIN Order AS o on c.customer_id = o.customer_id;
Explanation: the above statement creates a view named Customer_Orders that retrieves customers and joins the Order table to the list of data.

# Chapter 12 – Security and Users

**Chapter Objective:** Security should be one of the most important factors when working with database design. This chapter explains security and how to set up users to protect data from unauthorized access.

Good security is what separates your private data from being seen by the public. Hackers consistently want to gain access to a database server to steal data. Even spam hackers use database access to print content to your site without your knowledge. When you design your tables, you also need to design security for your website. This chapter will show you how to create users and permissions, and we'll give you tips on what you should do with your newly installed database layout.

**Reviewing Current Security**

Before you begin working with security and permissions, you need to review the way the database is set up. MySQL has a default security setup when you first install it.

Let's take a look at what you should do before you work with security and granting privileges. You first want to review a list of hosts and user names already installed on the machine. Take a look at the following SQL statement.

SELECT host, user, password FROM mysql.user;

The above statement gets a list of host, users and passwords from the system user table. Of course, you won't be able to see the passwords in plain text. The passwords are automatically encrypted using SQL's own internal engine.

You should see output similar to the below.

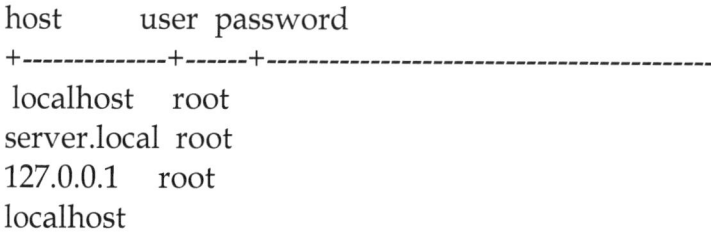

```
host       user  password
+-------------+------+----------------------------------------
 localhost    root
server.local  root
127.0.0.1    root
localhost
```

Notice your server has three host names: localhost, server.local and 127.0.0.1. The root user is associated with all three of these host names. You'll need these host names when you attempt to log in to the database server. Most administrators work with localhost, and then they assign user names to localhost for applications.

The root user name is the main administrator account that gives users full access to all database settings and security. In other words, you want to keep the root password extremely secure, and you don't want to give it to very many people within the company. If you work with the MySQL database, the root user will probably give you a separate user name and password to work with your own list of permissions.

One thing to note is that the root user name should never have an easy password or a blank password. Always assign a value to the root user's password, or you make it extremely easy for a third-party to gain access to the database.

## Creating Users

Now that you've viewed a list of users, you can determine what users you need to create for your database. In the above example, you just have the root user. This is common with a newly installed version of MySQL. Note that other databases use different naming conventions and features when assigning users to databases, but we're going to focus on MySQL and creating and assigning permissions on MySQL.

Before you create a new user, you should understand what privileges are needed. The most common reason you'll need to create a new user is for an application. Maybe the application uses a specific database, so you need to create a new user specific for the application and give the user privileges only to the application's relevant database. This means that if someone gets access to the user name, they only have access to the application's database and not the entire server.

Let's take a look at the SQL needed to create a new user.

CREATE USER 'myuser' @ 'localhost' IDENTIFIED BY 'password';

You'll notice a few customized values in the above statement. The CREATE USER phrase is specific to MySQL, and you need to type this part to create a user. The myuser is the name given to your user. The application and any users logging into the database server need this name.

If you aren't used to the way MySQL sets up users and access, the localhost part could be confusing. Since the localhost host name means the local server, your user can only log in to the database server named "localhost." Localhost is an internal name that means "the local server." This means that the user named myuser@localhost will always log in to the local database, and mysuser won't have access to any other database servers. In the list of other host names, you can also give myuser access to other host names, but it's not recommended especially if you're creating a user specifically for a database application.

The IDENTIFIED BY is then used to create a password for the user. In this example, the password of "password" is used, but you would not want to use this value since it's easily hacked. The MySQL database engine automatically encrypts this value and stores it in the system database. You always want to use SQL's encryption algorithms and store encrypted values in your tables. Plain text passwords put your users at risk in case the database is every hacked.

**Granting User Privileges**

You created a user named myuser, but the user still has access to nothing. If the user was to log in to the database server, they would not be able to query tables, create tables, delete data and tables or even review table architecture. For a user to be able to view these different database objects, you need to grant the user privileges. MySQL has a GRANT keyword that allows you to grant users privileges. There are several privileges you can grant, and they all have a different level of security risks.

The basic privileges you need to grant to a database application user is the read and write access to records. The application needs to retrieve data to read it, and it needs to use the UPDATE statement to change data. You need to specify to the MySQL database that the user can execute these statements on the database.

Let's take a look at a sample MySQL statement that you would use to grant access privileges to an application database user. Let's first take a look at the basic template command.

GRANT privileges ON object TO user;

The GRANT, ON, and TO keywords are specific to MySQL and necessary when you create the statement. The "privileges" section is the list of privileges you want to grant. Each privilege should be separated by a comma. The "object" section indicates the database object you want to give the user permissions to. For instance, if it's a table, you would use the table name. If you want to give the user access to the entire database, you specify the entire database object. You can give users object-level permissions, which makes your database much more secure from hackers.

Let's say you want to grant read, update and delete for a user named myuser. The following MySQL command is how you would grant permissions to your Customer table.

GRANT SELECT, UPDATE, DELETE ON Customer TO myuser @ localhost;

The above statement gives the myuser@localhost user access to read and write on the Customer table.

Let's say you want to get even more granular on your privileges. You can give specific access to columns within your table. For instance, you might want to only allow a user to read a customer's first name in the Customer table. You have social security numbers in the table, so you want to exclude this from the user's privileges.

The following SQL statement gives your user specific access to the customer's first name column only.

GRANT SELECT ON Customer.first_name TO myuser @ localhost;

The Customer's first name column is only accessible as a SELECT statement to myuser. This type of security is much more tedious for a database administrator to set up, but it's much more security for your database tables.

Let's say you want to give a user access to all privileges. Remember that creating users and providing users with access to objects are also privileges. Keep this in mind when you give all access privileges to a particular user.

Take a look at the following query to see how you can grant access to all objects for a user named myuser.

GRANT ALL PRIVILEGES ON Customer TO myuser @ localhost;

The above statement gives all privileges to your user. You can also give access to all database objects instead of specifying each one by one. The following statement gives a user named myuser access to all database objects with all possible privileges.

GRANT ALL PRIVILEGES ON *.* TO myuser @ localhost;

One thing to remember after you add permissions or change any of the security on your database: you must flush privileges and reload them. This can be done with one simple statement on the database server. The following statement shows you how to flush and reload MySQL privileges.

FLUSH PRIVILEGES;

Once you run the above statement, any permission changes are active including any new users and privileges recently created.

**Revoking Privileges**

Whether an employee leaves the company or you realize that you gave too much permissions for a specific user, there are times when you'll need to revoke privileges for a user. The SQL language gives you the ability to revoke or remove privileges on your database.

For instance, suppose that you didn't want to give a user DELETE permissions on the database. You've already flushed and reloaded permissions, but you want to change permissions and remove the DELETE option. The following SQL statement revokes privileges for a user.

REVOKE DELETE ON Customer FROM myuser @ localhost;

That's it. You've now removed the DELETE permission from the myuser user.

You can also choose to completely delete a user. This is beneficial when a database administrator leaves the company. You should ensure that the user name isn't being used by an application in any way before you remove the user.

However, deleting the user helps secure your database after the user no longer needs any permissions to tables or data.

The following command removes a user from the database.

DROP USER myuser @ localhost;

That's it. The user is gone and can no longer log in to your database.

This chapter showed you how to create users and grant them permission to different database objects. Security is important if you want to properly protect your business information.

**Lab Questions**

1. You determine that you need to create a user named myuser for your localhost database. Write the SQL statement to create the user.
CREATE USER 'myuser' @ 'localhost' IDENTIFIED BY 'password';
Explanation: This statement creates a user with an associated password for localhost.

2. You want to allow a user to retrieve data from a table named Order. Write the SQL statement that gives the user named myuser access.
GRANT SELECT ON Order TO myuser @ localhost;
Explanation: the above statement gives the user myuser SELECT permissions on the Order table.

3. What command do you use after you are finished changing permissions?
    a. ADD
    b. FLUSH PRIVILEGES
    c. ADD PRIVILEGES

d. REBOOT

Explanation: use the FLUSH PRIVILEGES command to reload privileges after you're finished with your configurations.

# Chapter 13 – Applications and SQL

**Chapter Objective:** Databases are used for dynamic page content in a cloud application. This chapter shows users how to use the basics such as connecting to a database and querying the database from PHP.

With some background information and understanding of SQL, you can then move forward with your first web page and application development. The next chapter focuses more on a website and PHP with SQL. In this chapter, we will get you started with linking your PHP pages with your MySQL database. MySQL works seamlessly with PHP, so it doesn't take much to set up the system. As long as you have Apache installed on your development machine, you can get started.

## PHP and SQL

As we already said, PHP and SQL are both compatible without much hassle. The most common environment used for PHP and SQL is called LAMP. LAMP stands for Linux, Apache, MySQL and PHP. This means that the most common way to set up a new SQL application is to use the Linux operating system with MySQL and Apache installed. With these two applications installed, you can run PHP applications.

One thing to note is the programming environment. With Apache you can run PHP files on a web server, but you still need a place to type your code. There are several different environments available. Some environments mix HTML and layouts with PHP such as Dreamweaver. You can use something as simple as Notepad++ for creating PHP files. Whatever you use, make sure you save any PHP files with the .php extension to ensure that your web server recognizes the file as an executable on the web server and not a static HTML page.

**Set Up the Database User**

Before you make a connection to the database from a PHP application, you want to ensure that you have a user set up on the MySQL database server. We covered how to create users and add privileges on the database in chapter 12, but let's go over what you need before you start working with PHP and SQL.

First, you need to ensure that the MySQL database is on the same development desktop that you are using for your PHP and Apache setup. While this isn't a requirement in the real-world, it will make troubleshooting and user permissions much easier. We will use the localhost host name in our examples, which means that when PHP attempts to connect to the database, it uses the local server where Apache is running. If you decide to put MySQL on a different server, you'll need to replace the localhost host name with your own MySQL database server's IP address or host name.

For our example, let's first create a user named myuser using the CREATE USER and GRANT SQL statement on the database.

Here is the syntax for creating a new user on your MySQL database server.

CREATE USER 'myuser' @ 'localhost' IDENTIFIED BY 'password';
GRANT SELECT, UPDATE, DELETE ON Customer TO myuser @ localhost;
GRANT SELECT, UPDATE, DELETE ON Order TO myuser @ localhost;

If you recall from the first chapter, the first SQL statement creates a user named myuser, and the user is given a password with the value of "password." This is, of course, not a viable password in the real world, but it's fine for a developer password that isn't available on the Internet.

The second line of code gives the user access to your Customer table. The second GRANT statement gives the myuser user access to the Order table. Since these are the two basic tables we've created and used throughout the lesson, we're going to use these two tables in our application.

Remember, you first need to flush privileges on the database before they take effect. After you run the above statements on your SQL server, type and run the following command.

FLUSH PRIVILEGES;

After you run this command, the user can now log in to the SQL server. You can verify by doing a SELECT on the MySQL system table. Type and run the following command to confirm that the new user named myuser is located in the list of users.

SELECT host, user, password FROM mysql.user;

If you recall from the previous chapter, the above statement lists all users in your database. You want to ensure that myuser @ localhost is located in the list of users. Once confirmed, you should not have any issues when you attempt to connect from your PHP application.

Once these statements are run on the database server, you can now connect to the database from your PHP application.

**Connecting to Your SQL Database**

Now it's time to switch to PHP code instead of SQL. Open your PHP programming environment such as Notepad++ for this next part. We need to create a file that connects to the SQL database. This file can be used throughout your entire application as the connection string for your database. These files are typically called includes when you're programming PHP pages.

First, you must enclose your include file with the PHP declarative statement. The enclosed statement tells the Apache server that you want to run backend, server side code instead of processing the PHP code as a static file. The following code must encapsulate all of your PHP code for your include page works on your server.

```
< ?
// your PHP statements go here
? >
```

With the above code in place, you can connect to your database. We'll go line by line to explain how the process works.

The first line of code sets your user name. Take a look at the following PHP statement.

```
$username = "myuser";
```

Notice that we use a dollar sign to indicate to the PHP language that we want to create a variable. Remember that SQL uses the @ character to indicate that you're creating a user defined variable. This is one difference between PHP and SQL. Notice, though, that we terminate the PHP statement in the same way we do with the SQL language. We terminate the statement with a semicolon.

In this example, we use the username variable to hold the user name for the database.

We have the user name variable, so now we need a password variable. Add the following PHP statement to your code.

```
$password="password";
```

This is the same password that we used when we created the myuser user. The format is the same, because we just want to store a string value to a PHP variable. Note that this value is not encrypted, so you want to keep your database PHP connection file secure from hackers.

The next variable we need is the database name. This tells the SQL engine what database it needs to query when you make a call to the database system.

```
$database="database";
```

Again, the format is the same since we just want to store the database name as a string value in PHP.

The next statement is different than the previous three. The next statement is the actual connection to the database.

This is an internal PHP function, so you don't need to perform any complex connection queries in PHP. PHP has this function already written with its internal system, so this is why working with MySQL and PHP is very convenient especially for new programmers.

Take a look at the following PHP statement.

mysql_connect(localhost,$user,$password);

The mysql_connect function takes three parameters. The first one is localhost. Remember that your myuser user is specific to localhost. The localhost host name tells the PHP engine to use the localhost database, which is the database on the local machine. You'll see that we use the user name and password variable in the function. This is needed so that the PHP engine can connect to the database without receiving an error.

With the connection set, now we can query the database. We'll use a simple query for this example, but you can create any one of the complex queries we've worked with in previous chapters to query the SQL server.

The following variable contains a simple SELECT statement.

$query = "SELECT first_name, last_name FROM Customer;";

With this query created, we use another internal PHP statement to send the query to the database.

mysql_query($query);

That's all it takes to query the database server. This one function is inherited in PHP, so you don't need to create any complex code. Just create the PHP string that contains the query and send it to the server with the above function. We'll get into parsing this information in the next chapter.

If there is any error with your user name and password, the original connect function should give you an error. The SQL function gives you a true or false response that you can use to detect if the connection was rejected. To add to your error handling, you can add a message to your code that's returned to the user when they attempt to connect through your application.

Let's take a look at the code for error handling.

```
$connected = mysql_connect(localhost,$user,$password);
if (!$connected) {
    echo "We could not connect to the server. Please try again.";
}
```

You'll notice that we still used the mysql_connect function, but this time we return a value. The value returned is true if the connection is successful, and it returns false if the connection fails. If you attempt to use the connection even after a failure, your code will fail. The above code is what is called error handling and sending a friendly message to the user. If the mysql_connect function returns false, then the next statement sends a message to your user to ensure that they understand an error occurred.

The final part of connection to a SQL server is to close the connection when you're finished.

This is an important part of programming SQL applications, because closing the connection frees up your web server's resources. If you have too many SQL connections open, the web server returns an error to your viewers.

After you complete your queries in PHP, it's time to close the connection. Use the following code at the end of your PHP code.

mysql_close();

Some programmers include this statement at the very end of each page in a separate include statement. You can use it in each page or make a separate include that is added to the end of each of your web pages.

This chapter showed you how to connect to a MySQL database in PHP. We also covered queries, but you still need to parse and show data to a web page. The next, final chapter covers your first "Hello World" web page.


## Lab Questions

1. You want to query the local host from a PHP application. Write the PHP function that makes the connection to a SQL database with a user name and password.
mysql_connect(localhost,$user,$password);
Explanation: The above statement connects to local host with the user name and password contained in the appropriate variables.

2. You've created a query in a variable named $query. Write the function that sends the query to the database.
mysql_query($query);

Explanation: this PHP function sends the query to the server and returns the results.

3. Once you've finished querying the database, write the function you need to free up database and web server resources.

```
mysql_close();
```

Explanation: this close method frees up resources and should be used with each of your PHP pages that use SQL.

# Chapter 14 – Your First Web Page

**Chapter Objective:** This chapter combines the knowledge of all previous chapters and gives you a hands on sample of writing your own web page. The objective is to understand how PHP and SQL work together to display results.

You've seen several SQL functions, logic and design. We also discussed connecting to your SQL server. Now, it's time to put all of the SQL coding into a practical example. It's common in the world of programming to show examples using the phrase "Hello World." Hello World is the common phrase given to someone's first program, because the idea is to give new programmers some hands on experience with writing a statement to the screen. In this case, we're going to write Hello World to the user's browser.

## Using PHP to Connect to the Database

The last chapter was dedicated to connecting to a SQL server, but it helps to step through the entire process again. We'll summarize the previous chapter to give you a refresher on connecting to the database. Remember that you need to set up a user name and password on your SQL server, and PHP has its own internal functions to connect and query to the database. You should also remember to close the connection once you're finished with querying.

Let's take a look at the code. This should be in an include fire at the top of your PHP page.

```
<?
$username = "myuser";
$password="password";
$database="database";
$connected = mysql_connect(localhost,$user,$password);
if (!$connected) {
    echo "We could not connect to the server. Please try again.";
}

?>
```

The above code sets up the user name and password and connects to the localhost database server. Remember that the localhost database server is the database engine running on the same machine as the web server. While this is not common on larger websites, it's common for development environments. If you have a separate SQL server on another machine, you need to replace localhost with the name of the MySQL database server or its IP address.

In the above example, we've also added some error handling, so if the database fails or the user no longer has access, a message is returned to the user without crashing your website.

## Querying the Database

With our database connection set up, we now need to query the database for information. In the previous sample, we decided to query the Customer table for a list of customers. We return the first and last name of the customer.

Let's take a look at the code again to query the Customer table.

$query = "SELECT first_name, last_name FROM Customer;";

You'll recognize the SELECT statement in the above string variable. We used the same SELECT statement in the previous chapter as well as the SELECT chapter where we showed you how to read data from a database.

The above PHP code just creates the query, but it doesn't actually query the database. We need to use the PHP internal function that queries the database. The mysql_query function does just that – it sends the query to the MySQL database.

Let's take a look at the code.

$result = mysql_query($query);

The above statement does the actual querying on the database. If the query is written without any syntax errors or mistakes, you'll receive a list of customers from the MySQL database in what is called a record set.

The difference between the previous chapter and this one is that we now store results in a variable named "result." All records are stored in an array as long as we have records to display. If there are no records to display, the $result variable has no records, and you won't be able to loop through them.

**Displaying Data to Users**

Now that you have your database connection and the query needed to get a list of customers, you need to set up your HTML page.

PHP works with HTML to display results from your tables. You need to place your PHP with HTML. The HTML code formats the data for your users. We will use a very simple HTML page to display data.

To set up your HTML, use the following code. Make sure you place this code outside of your encapsulating <? ?> PHP directives. PHP will throw an error otherwise. The following code creates a basic HTML template for you to use.

```
<html>
<head>
        <title>My First Page</title>
</head>
<body>
Customers <br/>

<?

?>
</body>
</html>
```

Notice that we inserted the PHP directives within the HTML's body tag. All of your printed text should be within the body tags in HTML. You can use any logic for your list of customers. For this example, we'll list each customer line by line.

Let's add some PHP code to the example.

```
<html>
<head>
        <title>My First Page</title>
</head>
<body>
```

Customers <br/>

```php
<?
$rows=mysql_numrows($result);
$i=0;
while ($i < $ rows) {

//SQL logic here

$i++;
}
?>
</body>
</html>
```

We've added quite a bit of code in the body tag. None of this code prints any data to the web browser, but it's important to understand the logic in this code.

The first PHP code gets the number of rows and assigns the value to $rows. Our Customer table only has 2 customers, so there should only be two rows returned. If your Customer table has 50 customers stored, you will have a row variable with the value of 50.

You might wonder why we need this value. This value is to loop through each record. The logic is that we have 2 rows, so we will loop through both of those records to retrieve the user's name. To successfully loop through a list of records, we first need to identify the number of records we have. If you excluded this logic, your PHP code will go through what is called an infinite loop. An infinite loop occurs when the PHP code continues to loop through records without the condition ever being met. Remember the cursor logic? We looped through each record. The "while" loop in the above code does the same thing, except the PHP code is much different.

The while loop has a condition set. This condition is what avoids an infinite loop in your PHP pages. An infinite loop crashes your pages and could crash your web server. In this condition, it says that once the $i variable is the same as the value in $rows, exit the loop. You'll see that the $i variable is incremented at each loop, so your while loop only loops 1 time.

Since our while loop doesn't really do anything except loop through records, let's include the logic that prints the customer's first name to the browser.

Here is the code with the loop logic included.

```
<html>
<head>
        <title>My First Page</title>
</head>
<body>
Customers <br/>
<?
$rows=mysql_numrows($result);
$i=0;
while ($i < $ rows) {

$first=mysql_result($result,$i,"first_name");
echo $first. "<br/>";

$i++;
}
?>
</body>
</html>
```

We added two more lines of code in our PHP loop. The first command uses the internal PHP mysql_results function, which is used to retrieve data from your data results. The function takes three parameters. The first one is the result set array. The next one is the $i variable. This variable tells PHP which array index to pull. Since the first array index is 0, the first record is pulled. When the loop increments the $i variable, the next array index is used, which is 1. Remember that arrays start at index 0, so an array with two records has values at index 0 and 1. This is one of the more difficult concepts for new programs to learn.

The echo statement is used to print a value to the browser. This statement just prints the value contained in the $first variable. Since the $first variable continuously changes as the array index is changed, this value is different for each loop.

The following is printed to your browser.

Customers
John
Jane

Notice that the names are placed on their own line. This is because we added a "<br/>" character to the end of each name. If we didn't add the break character to each line, you would get a line of names without any carriage returns. This is another point to remember when you're working with PHP and SQL data in a result set array.

**Sending Data to the Server**

We know how to retrieve data, but maybe we want to insert a new customer into the Customer table. We do this with an HTML form. Let's take a look at the code to create a form.

```
<html>
<head>
        <title>My First Page</title>
</head>
<body>
Enter your first name <br/>
<form action="insert.php" method="post">
First Name: <input type="text" name="first"><br>
<input type="Submit">
</form>
</body>
</html>
```

This form just asks the user for the first name. When the user clicks the submit button, you then need to retrieve the data with PHP and insert the new customer into the Customer table. Let's look at some example PHP code.

```
$first = $_POST['first'];
$query = "INSERT INTO Customer (first_name) VALUES ("'".$first."')";
mysql_query($query);
echo "Thank you";
```

Notice that the first variable from the form is then retrieved and placed into a variable named $firm. We used the same PHP functions we used earlier to send a query to the database, but we have no results returned when the database is simply inserting data into a table. Because we don't return results with an INSERT statement, we don't need to assign a return variable to the mysql_query function.

Put this code together and you have a form that submits to the page, inserts the record into the database, and displays a thank you message to the customer.

You've just written your first program in PHP and SQL. These two languages put together allow you to make complex applications for your website. Just remember to keep security as one of the most important parts of your database design when your application is open to the public. At this point, you've learned all the basic functionality of SQL and PHP code.

## Lab Questions

1. You want to get the number of rows returned from a SELECT query on the SQL database. Write the PHP code that returns the number of rows to a $rows variable.
$rows=mysql_numrows($result);
Explanation: in our example, only 2 records are returned, but you can have 0 or millions of rows stored in a data set.

2. You need to create a while loop to iterate through each row in your PHP code. Write the while statement you would use.
while ($i < $ rows) {
$i++;
}
Explanation: it's assumed that $i is set to 0 to start the loop, and then the loop continues to run until $i equals the number of rows.

3. What PHP command prints data to the browser window?
    a. echo
    b. print
    c. send
    d. post
Explanation: the echo statement prints data to the browser window including HTML to format the data.

# Conclusion

This book has found you because you have the ultimate potential.

It may be easy to think and feel that you are limited but the truth is you are more than what you have assumed you are. We have been there. We have been in such a situation: when giving up or settling with what is comfortable feels like the best choice. Luckily, the heart which is the dwelling place for passion has told us otherwise.

It was in 2014 when our team was created. Our compass was this – the dream of coming up with books that can spread knowledge and education about programming. The goal was to reach as many people across the world. For them to learn how to program and in the process, find solutions, perform mathematical calculations, show graphics and images, process and store data and much more. Our whole journey to make such dream come true has been very pivotal in our individual lives. We believe that a dream shared becomes a reality.

We want you to be part of this journey, of this wonderful reality. We want to make learning programming easy and fun for you. In addition, we want to open your eyes to the truth that programming can be a start-off point for more beautiful things in your life.

Programming may have this usual stereotype of being too geeky and too stressful. We would like to tell you that nowadays, we enjoy this lifestyle: surf-program-read-write-eat. How amazing is that? If you enjoy this kind of life, we assure you that nothing is impossible and that like us, you can also make programming a stepping stone to unlock your potential to solve problems, maximize solutions, and enjoy the life that you truly deserve.

This book has found you because you are at the brink of everything fantastic!

Thanks for reading!

You can be interested in: "Python: Learn Python In A DAY! - The Ultimate Crash Course to Learning the Basics of Python In No Time"

Here is our full library: http://amzn.to/1HPABQI

To your success,

Acodemy.

Made in the USA
Lexington, KY
15 April 2016